How to Land a Job in Journalism

PHIL SWANN • ED ACHORN

BETTERWAY PUBLICATIONS, INC.
WHITE HALL, VIRGINIA

Published by Betterway Publications, Inc.
Box 219
Crozet, VA 22932

Cover design by Tim Haley
Typography by East Coast Typography, Inc.

Library of Congress Cataloging-in-Publication Data

Swann, Phil
    How to land a job in journalism.

    Includes index.
    1. Journalism—Vocational guidance—Handbooks,
manuals, etc.   I. Achorn, Ed   II. Title.
PN4797.S94   1988   070′.02373   88-19401
ISBN 1-55870-101-X (pbk.)

Printed in the United States of America
0987654321

To Robert C. Achorn
and the memory of Lisa Marie Swann

Acknowledgments

We would like to express our deepest appreciation to the many journalists who took time out of their busy schedules to be interviewed for this book.

We also would like to thank Robert P. Clark for his wisdom and patience.

Lastly, we would like to extend a special thanks to Chris Achorn and Pat Maunsell for their help and encouragement during good times and bad. Without them, this book would not have been possible.

Foreword

by Robert P. Clark
Past President, American Society of Newspaper Editors

This is a *good* book.

You will like its style. It is breezy and bright. It is smooth-flowing and easy to read.

Most important, it contains really good advice.

I find its information sound, solid, and specific.

Furthermore, I don't think you can find this kind of information — certainly not in such a complete presentation — anywhere else.

I have asked several professors of journalism recently (a) if there were books on this subject and (b) if this kind of information was presented in any of the classes in their journalism schools.

The answers were (a) no, to the books and (b) well, some teachers may work some of this sort of material into their classes, or discuss it with students, but their schools had no organized presentations on it.

So this book should be a very valuable aid to students preparing for a job in journalism.

It also should be valuable to those who have graduated and are already at work but want to look elsewhere, and to those who have not yet found a job — or who have decided a few years after college that journalism, rather than what they are doing, may be their true life calling.

I have been asked countless times in my journalistic career for such advice as is in this book.

In fact in the past *month*, as I write this, four young people have asked me for help with their careers — one an editor looking for a new place; one a reporter searching for better opportunity elsewhere; one a recent journalism graduate (class of '87) wondering where to turn now; and one a freelance photographer wondering how and where to find a job in photojournalism.

I gave them much of the advice I have now read in this book. So I can give hearty endorsement to the information it contains.

Several years ago, in my first managing editorship — at *The Louisville Times* — I was recruiting for reporters at a nearby college. I was struck immediately by the prevailing attitude of the graduating seniors. It was, in effect, "What sort of job have you got for me?"

(In all fairness, it was a school without a journalism department but one where several students thought they might be interested in journalism careers.)

My attitude, on the other hand, was, "What have *you* got that should interest me in you?" Needless to say, I went away shaking my head and without a single prospect in mind for my newspaper.

I have interviewed many job candidates in my years as an editor — at colleges and universities, at Minority Job Fairs, and in my office after they wrote letters, with resumés and clips, that interested me.

I can tell you that every bit of advice in this book is in sync with my feelings and experience: that the application letter and the resumé are of paramount importance (that they must be neat, accurate, and pertinent); that working experience of some sort, whether on a college newspaper or an internship, is essential; that good editors these days are looking for broad educational backgrounds, not just journalistic skills; that willingness to work hard and eagerness to learn are definite pluses in this business; that the beginning journalist should get all the basic experience he can from a job before jumping to the next location. And so forth.

But *you* read the book for all the details.

It may be one of the most important, as well as most enjoyable, things you have ever done.

Contents

Chapter 1

Against All Odds?

HOW DO I LAND A JOB IN JOURNALISM?

Marc Stern at 26 was not a happy young man. He was losing interest in law school. His job at the local bank was numbingly dull.

"I just couldn't believe life could be so bleak," he recalls.

But, after months of soul searching, he knew what he had to do about it. Come what may, he was going to be a newspaper journalist.

"I was going to make an all-out effort to get into newspapers, sort of a do-or-die effort," Stern says. "It just seemed that nothing else would be meaningful. Anything else would seem like a nine-to-five job."

Stern, the son of the late Laurence Stern, a top *Washington Post* reporter, came equipped for the job hunt with great contacts — but no training or experience. He soon learned it wasn't enough. The *Post's* executive editor, Benjamin Bradlee, offered him some advice for getting his foot in the door ("ask for a job as a copy editor — reporters are a dime a dozen") but no position. After weeks of editors' snubs and unpromising interviews, Stern decided a journalism night course at a nearby college might at least flesh out his resumé. Undaunted by the fact that the class was full, he persuaded the teacher — the managing editor of a 14,000-circulation daily in California — to allow him to sit in one night as an observer. When that night came, he went for broke.

He made his teacher an offer he couldn't refuse. Though Stern was married and the father of a young child, he asked to work at the teacher's newspaper forty hours a week as a copy editor — for free.

The astonished editor didn't need much time to mull over Stern's offer.

"He wouldn't let me into his class, but he let me be a slave at his newspaper," Stern recalls with a laugh.

11

Stern had no paycheck, but he had one foot in the door. After several weeks of long hours on the copy desk, the editor put him on the payroll. And within three years, Stern was working as a reporter in the Washington bureau of Copley Newspapers, the chain that owns that 14,000-circulation paper.

Stern paid his dues, but he never regretted his gamble.

"I think that really illustrates the kind of risk and sacrifice people have to make if they want to get into this business," Stern says. "You've got to be an ambitious, driven person to carry yourself through the first couple of years when you're garbage."

Of course, not everyone has to toss in free labor to win that first job as a reporter, copy editor, or news photographer. There are as many stories about breaking in as there are journalists. Some people get hired by hanging around the news room when they are still in school, graduating to copy boys and then reporters. Some work as $15-a-night stringers or peddle freelance photos for months before getting chances. Some go to journalism school, work for their student newspapers, get internships, and convince editors they've got the guts and smarts to be full-time employees.

But as varied as those stories are, they almost invariably teach the same basic lessons about landing a job in journalism:

It's Not Always Easy, But You Can Do It

You'll face competition for good newspaper jobs because thousands of people have discovered journalism is one of the best gigs ever invented. Fairly sane people are willing to forgo big salaries, fantastic perks, and regular hours to spend their lives doing a job that is both fascinating and important. Journalists make a real difference in people's day-to-day lives; in a dangerous world, their freedom and happiness depend on the job journalists do. That's why newspaper jobs are treasured positions. You may have a fight on your hands.

Information is Power

Learn as much as you can about newspapers and the job hunt. You will increase your chances of getting the job you want.

Experience is Golden

Show an editor you can cut the mustard. Work for the college newspaper. Get an internship. And when you graduate, be willing to take a job that may not be your first choice just to get your foot in the door.

Contacts are Invaluable

Get to know some people in the business. Their advice is often terrific, and one of them may offer you a job someday.

You Will Have to Pay Your Dues

When your former school chums are mulling stock options or buying bigger houses, you may be counting your change to see if you can get fries with your hamburger. There are few overnight success stories. And, while the salaries are excellent at the nation's top newspapers, the competition for those jobs is fierce.

It Helps if You Have a Fire in the Belly for the Business

There are easier and less demeaning ways to begin earning a living. Your job hunt may test whether you have a thick enough skin to handle rejection and a big enough heart to keep struggling when your chances look bleak.

But don't panic. You can do it! And we want to help.

HOW WILL THIS BOOK HELP?

We've collected practical no-nonsense tips from scores of journalists from newspapers of all sizes published all over the country. We'll take you — step by step — through the techniques that helped them and their colleagues. We'll show you the classic pitfalls of young journalists who just can't seem to grab an editor's attention, and the tricks that help their successful peers.

You'll learn what you can do months before the job hunt to give yourself a big jump on the competition. We'll show you how to make the most effective use of your experience and personality. We'll go over the basics — how to write a terrific resumé, how to grab an editor with a cover letter, how to dress for an interview.

We think you'll be surprised, as we were, by how sensible and simple these techniques are — and by the fact you've never thought of them before.

Though we address the book primarily to aspiring newspaper reporters, it will also help those interested in becoming copy editors or photojournalists. In fact, we think anybody already in the business will have an easier time moving up the ladder after reading it.

We won't kid you. These insider tips alone will not win you the job of your dreams. You've got to stir in the most important ingredients: talent and persistence. But if you're serious about breaking into newspapers, this book can dramatically increase your chances of success. There is a good newspaper job for every talented, tenacious applicant reading these words.

BUT ISN'T IT TOUGH TO GET A JOB AT A NEWSPAPER?

Each year, thousands of applications from talented, highly educated young prospects wind up in the hands of editors. Many editors can sit back and pick the very best, the ones who make a newspaper shine.

"That's how you become a great editor: get a helluva lot of good people working for you," says Don Marsh, editor of *The Charleston (WV) Gazette*, which has a circulation of more than 100,000 on Sunday. "We get all sorts of people with impressive journalism backgrounds. I've hired people from the Columbia Journalism School, Princeton, and Yale."

"I don't get a lot of turnover and I get tons of applications. I may hire only three people a year at (the beginning) level," says Will Fehr, editor of *The Salt Lake Tribune*, which has a Sunday circulation of more than 130,000.

"It's a buyer's market. We can pick out the really top-notch people. We'd be damned fools if we didn't," says John Lemmon, managing editor of *The (Baltimore) Evening Sun*, circulation 175,000.

It's a sweet deal — for those editors. From the other side of the resumé, of course, the picture looks bleaker.

But don't throw away your dreams yet. Getting a good newspaper job is a challenge, but it's not a Herculean task.

In general terms, competition for jobs stiffens in proportion to the circulation of the paper. So, while it is next to impossible for a college graduate to step into a job at a large metropolitan daily, his or her chances aren't half bad at a 30,000-circulation paper. Competition for jobs at dailies tends to be tougher on the East and West coasts than in America's Midwest and the Plains. Job availability depends greatly on a region's economic conditions, population fluctuations, local newspaper competition, and the proximity of the paper to universities and journalism programs.

Art Cullen, managing editor of the 10,600-circulation *Ames (IA) Daily Tribune*, says he is fortunate his paper is based in the home town of Iowa State University. He says the college's journalism program provides him a steady supply of top-notch applicants. By contrast, his former paper, an 8,000-circulation weekly in Algona, roughly 100 miles north, was "just begging for help," he says.

Cullen says many young journalists make the mistake of thinking, "You are not a human being unless you work for the big daily in the big city . . . It's very difficult to get people in rural areas."

"It's not that difficult to get a job (at smaller newspapers) in Nebraska," says Ruth John, a personnel officer in charge of recruiting for the *Omaha World Herald*, which has a daily circulation of more than 200,000.

Midwestern university journalism placement programs in recent years report placing many May graduates in jobs before Christmas. Even on the East and West coasts, editors of small dailies are interested in — instead of merely inundated by — applications from beginning journalists.

"It's getting harder and harder to find applicants," says Carl E. Beck Jr., former editor of the *Press-Enterprise*, a 22,000-circulation daily in Bloomsburg, PA.

"If other papers in Oregon are, like me, getting fewer and fewer applications, then when an application does come in from somebody who looks fairly promising, we certainly pay attention to that," says Mike Forrester, editor of the *East Oregonian*, a 12,500-circulation daily. "It means more to me than it did ten years ago . . . I'm much more happy to get that."

So while competition for good newspaper jobs tends to be fierce, opening positions are available. Look for the situationsand newspapers that seem to give you the best preparation for a bright future. (More on that later.)

This book should improve your chances of getting a job in any area.

You may not, however, be hired to the job you covet the day after you graduate. According to the Dow Jones Newspaper Fund, a foundation that encourages young people to enter journalism, approximately 46 percent of the journalism and mass communications graduates in 1987 either took jobs in non-media fields, went back to school, or remained unemployed four to five months after leaving school.

But 54 percent of graduates were hired. Many of them went into television, radio, trade publications, or newsletters, but about 40 percent of them got daily or weekly newspaper jobs. That means about 4,000 graduates were hired by newspapers shortly after graduation.

The Dow Jones study also shows that a journalism or mass communications major who took several news editorial courses had a dramatically better chance of landing a newspaper job than someone else who took advertising, public relations, or television and radio.

So if you are a journalism or mass communications major — especially if you are taking news editorial courses — the odds are good that you will land a newspaper job. But clearly the number of candidates is greater than the number of jobs. And today's graduates enter the job search competing against better trained people than ever before. In 1960, the *Columbia Journalism Review* reports, 10,349 students were enrolled in undergraduate journalism programs. That figure had jumped eight times by the late 1980s.

The newspaper business is highly competitive. But you should expect that. Any job worth having is worth fighting for. And there are jobs available.

BUT WHY DO SOME PEOPLE GET JOBS WHILE OTHERS FAIL?

The Dow Jones statistics provide some answers:

Experience

Approximately 80 percent of graduates hired for daily newspaper jobs had experience working on their college newspapers. And nearly 80 percent had internships — or journalism-related jobs — during school. More than a quarter of those interns were hired by the companies for which they worked while in college.

Internships are so valuable that candidates scrap almost as hard for them as for jobs. The Atlanta *Constitution* once received 300 applications for twelve spots in a ten-week internship program.

Education

Virtually all new hires are college graduates. We're not suggesting you can't get a newspaper job if you don't have a college degree. Many people, including some of the best journalists in the country, never graduated from college. But a degree — particularly a major in journalism — helps in the job hunt. And, of graduates getting daily newspaper jobs, 85 percent were journalism or mass communications majors.

Grades

About 95 percent of journalism graduates hired by daily newspapers reported getting senior year grades of B-minus or higher. Few editors decide to hire someone just because of grades, but few ignore them.

An Early Start

Approximately 30 percent of graduates who landed jobs with daily newspapers started looking four months before graduation. More than half of the success stories started looking at least two months before graduation. The figures are similar for graduates who won jobs in broadcasting.

WHAT ARE THE JOB PROSPECTS FOR MINORITIES?

They are generally good and getting better. Newspaper officials openly admit, though, that prospects were terrible in the past. They say the industry has had to make a concerted effort to improve.

Threatened by anti-discrimination suits, communication companies are actively seeking to hire and promote more people who define themselves as blacks, Hispanics, Asians or Pacific Americans, native Americans or native Alaskans. The white males in power are also hiring more women for top management spots, traditionally a white male domain.

For example, the number of minority employees in American news rooms jumped from 400 in 1968 to 3,400 in 1986; the number of women's names on the mastheads of the five largest dailies went from zero in 1961 to eleven in 1986.

The threat of lawsuits is not the only driving force behind the change. Many editors have concluded that their papers are stronger if they have people from varied backgrounds in the news room.

Large chains of newspapers are now issuing marching orders to their member papers to improve "the number" of minorities in the news room. Editors at large metropolitan dailies say top minority candidates have the edge over their non-minority counterparts for the time being.

F. Gilman Spencer, editor and senior vice president of the *New York Daily News,* a paper which in 1987 settled a multi-million dollar discrimination suit out of court, says when he looks at a resumé package, "If it's black, I'm interested already."

While this effort to catch up quickly may throw some roadblocks in front of white males — particularly for higher paying jobs up the ladder — statistics show that non-minority journalism graduates still get about nine out of every ten starting jobs. There is a long way to go before the numbers of minorities in the news room reflect the numbers in society as a whole, a goal of the industry by the year 2000.

Recent statistics show some progress. Daily and weekly newspapers hired about 14 percent of the minority graduates of journalism schools in 1985, compared to 3 percent in 1975.

Numerous scholarships and internships are now geared to minorities.

Women, meanwhile, appear to have little problem getting entry-level jobs. There are about 1.4 female graduates who majored in news-editorial for every one male graduate; they win jobs at daily and weekly newspapers by roughly the same margin over male graduates.

For more information about minorities in journalism, you can write for:

• *Help is Available!* Single copy free. Available from the American Society of Newspaper Editors, Minority Affairs Director, P.O. Box 17004, Washington, DC 20041.

• *Newspaper Journalism . . . For Minorities.* Second Edition. Single copy free, two or more copies 75 cents each. Available from Director, Division of Journalism, Florida A & M University, Tallahassee, FL 32307.

• *Journalism Career Guide for Minorities.* Single copy free. Lists minority scholarships offered by schools, newspaper internships and grants by the industry, participants at minority recruiting fairs, and tips for landing a job and planning a career. Published by the American Newspaper Publishers Foundation, the American Society of Newspaper Editors, the Associated Press Managing Editors Association, the Dow Jones Newspaper Fund, Inc., and the Society of Professional Journalists, SDX. Their addresses are:

American Newspaper Publishers Association Foundation
P.O. Box 17407
Dulles International Airport
Washington, DC 20041

American Society of Newspaper Editors
P.O. Box 17004
Washington, DC 20041

The Dow Jones Newspaper Fund, Inc.
P.O. Box 300
Princeton, NJ 08543-0300

The Society of Professional Journalists, SDX
53 W. Jackson Blvd., Suite 731
Chicago, IL 60604

ARE TRENDS CHANGING NEWSPAPER JOBS? WILL NEWSPAPERS STILL BE AROUND IN 40 YEARS?

For a time, doomsayers were prophesying the death of the American newspaper. They predicted that the reader, equipped with a modem and a computer, would get his news on a television monitor instead of picking up the paper on his doorstep. They pointed to the numbers of big city papers dying like flies as advertisers shoveled their dollars into television. They argued that the communications revolution, speeding up service and making storage of facts easier, would wipe out the need for the multitude of papers that stretch across the continent. They said vampire-like free "shoppers" would suck away enormous amounts of ad revenues from real newspapers, draining their lifeblood.

They were wrong. Oh, some people are reading news on computer monitors and some dailies have died. But the reader is not a machine. He likes the "human touch" of a folded newspaper in a coffee shop or a subway train. He likes to read local news about his school and friends and children. He feels a newspaper gives him a breadth and depth that TV news usually doesn't. And he is reluctant to read some flyer in his mailbox that has nothing but advertising in it. He wants news.

The death of scores of newspapers didn't spell the doom of the industry. There are around eighty fewer daily newspapers than in 1961. But the paid circulation of the nation's newspapers has actually climbed nearly four million since then, according to the *Columbia Journalism Review*. Meanwhile, total revenues have doubled: $12.7 billion in 1961 to about $26 billion now. Some competition between papers died, and readers probably suffered for it. But the American newspaper industry as a whole remained healthy and powerful — and will continue to produce good jobs for the foreseeable future. The number of daily print jobs won by journalism graduates, for example, has held steady at about 3,100 a year for the last ten years.

One reason for that is the growth of the suburban newspaper. As readers made their homes in the suburbs, they found the need to supplement their metropolitan daily with a suburban daily or weekly paper so they could get the local news the big city paper ignores. Suburban papers offer some exciting prospects for beginning journalists.

Thanks to another striking trend in the industry, chances are greater than ever before that starting reporters will work for a newspaper chain. Chain-owned dailies accounted for 46.1 percent of the total circulation of U.S. dailies in 1961. That figure climbed to around 80 percent by the late 1980s. Job applicants must look not only at newspapers, but the groups that own them.

This trend will surely affect you. Family-owned newspaper publishers typically care about their employees more than this era's distant, gray business people who look only at the bottom line. Some chains are moneymaking machines dominated by small and lackluster newspapers. But others are committed to quality journalism and to their employees. Executives at the best chains will reach down to their smaller papers for good people to promote to their bigger and better ones or to their top bureaus. A first-rate group could give you a head start on a first-rate career.

A changing society has also changed the kind of jobs available at newspapers. Studies say readers want splashier lifestyle pages, more color graphics, more sports than ever, more interesting stories about investment opportunities and entrepreneurs who "struck it rich," more health and environment stories, more reporting about the media itself, and more commentary and analysis of the news. An applicant who has a special expertise in one or more of these areas may have an edge on the competition.

An increase in newspaper libel suits may also be making itself felt on the job market. There is a strong demand for good copy editors — those special people willing to slave over copy for hours each day to make sure it is free from glaring mistakes or unanswered questions. And as papers perform more of their production right in the news room, instead of at a pasteup board, desk editors who have an art background will be increasingly in demand.

Newspapers will continue to change. We are clearly in the infancy of a communications revolution. But it appears the reader will always want news collected, edited, and transmitted by people who know what they are doing. And he will probably want to fold the newspaper under his arm and carry it around with him.

HOW WELL DOES JOURNALISM PAY?

We'll let the headline of a story in the *Washington Journalism Review* do the talking: "Life on the Bottom Rung; Pauper's Pay in the Fourth Estate." The grim news you've heard is true. If you want to raise a family early in your career, you might want to marry someone who works in a business that pays well.

"We are not paying reporters a living wage," says Tucker Sutherland, president of Sutherland Media, a Texas-based company that owns newspapers and magazines. "In many cases, without parental help or a working spouse, reporters lack enough money for the bare necessities."

Sutherland says he once considered cutting costs by hiring secretaries to perform some of the reporters' duties — until he found that secretaries earn 18 percent more than reporters.

You'll have to factor in a poor salary when you search for a job, and perhaps scratch some areas off your list because you cannot afford to live there.

"Starting reporters cannot afford to live in Norwalk, Connecticut," says William Neubeck, former managing editor of *The Hour* in Norwalk, and now an editor for the *Asbury Park Press* in New Jersey. "The minimum rent for the barest accommodations would cost an individual $400 a month, and at $245 (the paper's salary for starting reporters), you can't afford that . . . It is now almost required that (*The Hour*) either hire reporters from the weeklies in the county who are already living here or the sons and daughters of families in the area because they at least have a place to live."

Many journalists, including the authors of this book, lived at home when they started working for newspapers.

"We start people at $240 (and) we expect people to be erudite, but we expect them to come in at service station attendants' wages. It's shameful," says Don James, editor of the *Wichita Falls (TX) Times Record-News*, which has a Sunday circulation of nearly 50,000. "I've got two brothers in the garage business and they're making more money than I am."

Why is that?

Rolfe Neill, publisher of *The Charlotte (NC) Observer*, sums it up.

"I love my job. I'd do it for nothing. I can't wait to get out of my bed in the morning to get to work every day," Neill says.

Working for a newspaper is a great job. For many people, a lifetime of financial sacrifice is worth the constantly changing challenge that journalism provides. That's why so many people go into the business. And that's why newspaper publishers, despite occasional pangs of guilt, pay journalists dirt-poor rates. Publishers of small papers who sweat to squeeze out small profit margins have had little incentive to pay higher salaries. Anyone who didn't like it could take a hike. There was always an applicant ready to step in and work like a dog.

However, many editors of small papers are concerned that

young people will turn to other careers if they do not raise salaries soon. They are alarmed by studies indicating that a growing number of students are abandoning news editorial for public relations or advertising.

Some surveys show that entry-level salaries are rising, apparently in response to this trend. Nevertheless, the median starting salary in 1985 was a paltry $13,520 or $260 a week. That's tough for a student who has college loan payments hanging over his head.

The American Society of Newspaper Editors (ASNE) found that starting reporters earn significantly less than starting teachers, who work nine months a year and have won widespread public sympathy for being grossly underpaid. The wretched pay of reporters — who play a vital role in a free society — goes all but unnoticed outside the news rooms of America.

The smaller the paper, the smaller the starting salary tends to be. Papers with circulations of 50,000 to 100,000 paid starting reporters an average of $16,224, according to a 1986 ASNE survey. Papers with circulations of 5,000 or less paid $10,816 a year. Photographers tended to fare slightly worse.

Journalists do better as they climb the ladder, though they still lag behind other professions. The ASNE survey found that reporters working at 250,000-plus circulation papers who have five years of newspaper experience earned an average of $35,412 a year. Top reporters at the same sized papers earned an average of $41,808. Five-year reporters at 50,000 to 100,000 circulation papers earned an average of $24,440, according to the survey.

The average salary for an editor at a 100,000 to 250,000-circulation paper was $93,222. The average for an editor of a 10,000 to 18,000-circulation daily was $32,672. Senior editors at the nation's largest papers earn hundreds of thousands of dollars a year, a salary comparable with the rest of the corporate world.

The 1986 survey also reflects the demand for copy editors. Starting copy editors earned roughly $1,000 more a year than starting reporters.

Certainly, low profits are not the main reason for the pay squeeze. Newspaper analysts note that many small papers, enjoying profit margins of 25 to 30 percent, could afford to pay reporters more.

Ponder carefully before you choose a career in journalism.

If you decide to go ahead, use all the ammunition available — including this book — to land a job with the biggest and best paper possible and then move up further. It means thousands of dollars to you.

Of course, salaries are sometimes not the only financial incentive. Some newspaper companies sweeten the pot with profit-sharing plans. But, hopefully, the trend towards higher pay will continue so the business does not suffer a brain drain in the coming years.

WHAT IF I WANT TO BAIL OUT OF NEWSPAPER JOURNALISM AT SOME POINT?

Many people do. Even if newspapers pay poorly, newspaper experience is often viewed as a valuable commodity outside of the industry. Companies need to communicate with each other and the public, and they know newspaper people are trained to tell a story quickly and succinctly.

Newspaper experience can put you in line for some lucrative and interesting work:

Corporate Public Relations

In recent years, corporations have placed a growing emphasis on their image. They often hire people with working experience in journalism because they know how the press thinks and acts. Newspaper people often know how to best communicate a corporation's point of view.

Lobbying

Lobbyists work at communicating their client's views on issues. They also gather information about the political climate and report back to their clients. Newspaper experience is good training for that field.

Newsletters

In an increasingly complex and diverse society, people need specialized information. Newsletters focusing on everything from prescription drugs to doll furniture are riding a rocket of explosive growth. Money can be made in this field, and journalists have dropped out of newspaper reporting to grab some.

Teaching

Many journalism school professors are drawn from the ranks of the working press.

Government

Politicians and government workers must know how to communicate their ideas succinctly. Newspapers have served as a training ground for many in that profession, including Senators Paul Simon of Illinois and Albert Gore of Tennessee and former President John F. Kennedy, who put in a brief stint as a reporter after World War II.

Photography

If you are a photojournalist, you will always be in demand — for portraits, public relations shots, and a variety of other possibilities.

Government Public Relations

State and federal government agencies, and some local government offices, often hire journalists to handle their media relations. Thousands of such jobs exist in Washington and the fifty states' capitals.

Broadcasting

Lou Grant is not so unusual. Many newspaper reporters and editors make the jump from print to broadcast journalism, and sometimes jump back.

A WORD TO OUR READERS IN BROADCAST JOURNALISM

Though this book refers to newspaper journalism — specifically reporting — the same techniques that win jobs in that competitive business also win jobs in broadcast journalism.

Obviously, there are some differences. Though your resumé and application will be much the same, you will submit an audio or videotape of broadcasts to an editor instead of clips. The same basic approach holds, though. Send about six examples of your best work to a news editor. Strive — as you would with newspaper clippings — to submit interesting and varied work. Feature material that transcends locality (see Chapter Four). Submit a tape with your resumé, and don't expect to get it back; that will give you an edge over a competitor who doesn't want to invest in a tape, and does so only if an editor asks for one. Often that applicant waits for a request that never comes. Make it easy for the editor to become familiar with your work.

For the most part, though, we believe the advice here makes a graceful leap from print to broadcast journalism. We hope you will find our tips helpful.

For more information about careers in broadcast journalism, write for:

• *Careers in Broadcast News.* Single copy free with stamped (45 cents) self-addressed six-by-nine envelope. Available from Radio Television News Directors Association, 1735 DeSales Street, N.W., Washington, DC 20036.

• *Careers In Cable.* $3.50. Handbook providing a descriptive history of career opportunities in the cable industry. Available from the National Cable Television Association, 1724 Massachusetts Avenue, Washington, DC 20036.

• *Careers In Radio.* $1 per copy prepaid. Available from the Publications Department, National Association of Broadcasters, 1771 N Street, N.W., Washington, DC 20036.

• *Careers in Television.* $1 per copy prepaid. Available from the same address as *Careers in Radio.*

• *Women on the Job: Careers in the Electronic Media.* Single copy free. Available from American Women in Radio and Television Inc., 1321 Connecticut Avenue, N.W., Washington, DC 20036, or Women's Bureau, U.S. Department of Labor, 200 Constitution Avenue, N.W., Washington, DC 20010.

Chapter 2

Going For It!

DO I NEED TO WORK IN COLLEGE TO PREPARE FOR A CAREER IN JOURNALISM?

Imagine you are at your first interview. The editor is one of those hard-boiled types who doesn't worry about how he parts his hair because he parted ways with it a long time ago — worrying about his newspaper. His voice is as gravelly as the grounds of a drive-in theater because of the hundreds of times he's yelled across the news room on deadline. He broke in at the paper when he was twenty years old for $65 a week, and loves to talk about the time he scooped *The New York Times*. Is there anything more important to him than his newspaper? His family — but sometimes it takes a back seat.

And now you are in the hot seat.

Let's say your resumé suggests you've been missing in action the last four years. No writing courses. No internships. And you didn't even read the campus newspaper, much less work for it. Your GPA? It was BAD.

What are your chances?

The editor may consider you if he's running a small publication and needs someone yesterday. But he will treat you like yesterday's news if there's another applicant who has already demonstrated a commitment to the business.

Why?

Reporting the news fairly and accurately is just as serious as practicing law, medicine, or any other trade in which there is no room for error. Make one mistake and the reader may question every story in the paper. The editor wants someone who will get it right the first time and every time.

Can you convince him that you have the right stuff if you've never written a news story before?

"We think it's a real gamble to hire somebody right out of college because we don't know how they're going to perform and even they don't know," says John Carroll, editor of the *Lexington (KY) Herald-Leader*, a morning daily which has a circulation of more than 100,000.

Sure, a good editor expects and even looks forward to training a new reporter, copy editor, or photographer. He enjoys molding a young journalist in his image. But he can't shape something out of nothing. Give him something to work with.

When one of your authors was a student at the University of Maryland, a friend switched his major to journalism in his junior year. But he did not seek an internship or work for the college newspaper during his final two years. Upon graduation, he sent resumés to dozens of papers but received enough rejection letters to wallpaper his home.

Several months later, he came to the end of his rope. He gave up and took a job as a truck driver for a local supermarket chain. Friends joked he had developed a need to be close to food.

He didn't have much of a chance without practical experience or clips. But he never understood this and hid behind the usual excuses: "They want somebody from an Ivy League college . . . You can't get anywhere without connections . . . There are no jobs in this business."

At last report, he was still driving a truck.

"You have to have something to show your ability," warns James King, retired editor of *The Seattle Times,* an evening newspaper which has a circulation of about 230,000. "If they failed to go to a weekly or a small daily for a summer job, where do they find themselves? Way behind."

Okay, you don't have to work every waking hour in college to get ahead. Some people with little or no journalism experience get hired. But put the odds in your favor! Get the best job you can! Show that you want to work for a newspaper more than anything else. You will likely interview with an editor who displayed that burning desire when he was in college. And an editor — any employer — tends to hire someone who reminds him of himself.

"When I went into journalism, I wanted a job at a newspaper and the last thing I even asked was how much am I going to get paid," recalls King, a veteran of more than four decades in newspapers. "I wanted a job."

Remember, it doesn't take much to drive a bread truck, but it takes drive to be a journalist. What you do in school will largely determine where you work, for whom, and for how much.

"It's an awful lot of hard work," says Claude Sitton, vice president and editorial director of *The News and Observer* in Raleigh, NC, which has a Sunday circulation of nearly 180,000. "If you're not willing to do it, sell shoes."

But if you are willing, your friends will want to be in your shoes. You will have a great job.

WHAT SHOULD I DO IN COLLEGE? WHAT COURSES SHOULD I TAKE?

Editors want well-rounded individuals, not just "journalism junkies." Yes, you should know how to write and edit a news story. But an editor likes a young journalist to be active, curious, perhaps to have interests as varied as the Laffer Curve and the split-finger fast ball.

Why?

An editor dreams of discovering a diamond in the rough. When he looks across his desk during the interview, he wonders whether the applicant has the talent and ambition to someday be his best business reporter, science writer, political analyst, or copy editor. He knows he has something special if the job seeker majored in journalism, minored in chemistry, worked at the college newspaper, was president of the Debate Club, and had an internship at a local business publication.

You don't have to be a Jack or Jill of all trades to fetch a simple job at a newspaper. The ability to write a story with a strong angle is more important than the ability to add an isosceles triangle.

But use the time in college to boost your stock, to get the best job possible after graduation. If you can show an interest in a variety of subjects, an editor might think you can handle any beat in the news room or edit any story that comes across your desk.

Versatility will not only make you more attractive to your first employer, but more valuable later in your career. For example, an editor would be more likely to give you a plum assignment on the business page if you have an economics minor.

"How can you cover the environmental story if you've never had chemistry or biology?" asks Claude Sitton of *The Raleigh News and Observer*.

Today's accredited journalism programs are aimed at producing well-rounded applicants. An accredited journalism college currently requires at least ninety semester hours outside of journalism courses, with at least sixty-five of these in the liberal arts and sciences. In general terms, there should be a 75-25 percent split between non-journalism and journalism classes. Editors suggest you make the most of your liberal arts education and take a wide variety of courses, ranging from economics to science to government.

Also, get involved in as many extracurricular activities as possible and note them in your resumé. Make that resumé jump out of the pile. John Carroll of the *Lexington Herald-Leader* recalls that he once hired a copy editor because she had a Ph.D. in entomology. He was impressed that she had mastered such a difficult subject.

"The key is to have something special going for you," says William German, executive editor of the *San Francisco Chronicle*, which has more than half a million readers.

How do you get tagged with that "special" label? Sorry, there's no model for you to follow. John Carroll might like entomology, but another editor might wonder why you like bugs.

But you can't go wrong if you show an interest in a variety of subjects. And if you're thinking about a minor, try economics or science. Good business and science writers are always in demand.

"One of the best things a student can do is to become a specialist in the field," says William Block, president and publisher of the *Pittsburgh Post-Gazette,* a morning paper which has a circulation of approximately 168,000. "I don't care if it's the sex life of the honeybee. Sooner or later, it's going to be useful."

Editors also suggest you take as many writing courses as possible — particularly if you are not a journalism major. They don't have to be journalism courses. Creative writing, English, history , political science, and countless others can help develop your writing and research skills. Find out if a course will require extensive writing before you sign up.

SHOULD I MAJOR IN JOURNALISM?

A journalism major gives you a leg up on the competition, but is not absolutely required. Many editors say it's not as important as an internship, good clips, and practical experience. An English major with two internships and a regular job on the school paper has a much better chance of landing a job than a journalism major who sat on his behind for four years.

Many editors and reporters, including one of your authors, are not journalism school graduates. Seymour Hersh, whose expose of the My Lai massacre made history, was a history major. F. Gilman Spencer, editor and senior vice president of the (New York) *Daily News,* and investigative reporter Carl Bernstein of Watergate fame never even graduated from college.

"I have a science degree and I value that very much," says N. Christian Anderson, editor of *The Orange County (CA) Register,* which has a daily circulation of more than 300,000. "I took things like anthropology and history."

Nevertheless, statistics show that the overwhelming majority of new hires are journalism majors. Clearly, it is a big plus. John Lemmon, managing editor of *The (Baltimore) Evening Sun,* says journalism school helps a recent graduate "to hit the ground running. He doesn't have to go through the process of learning a lot of the basic things that a graduate of a good journalism school would know."

Majoring in journalism is not etched in stone. But you may run into a stone wall unless you learn the fundamentals somehow — an internship, the school paper, or journalism college. Preferably, you should do all three, although that is not required.

"If they did not have a journalism degree, it would be essential that they had some practical work at the college newspaper or an internship," says Dick Tarpley, retired editor of the *Abilene Reporter-News* (TX).

Don James, editor of the *Wichita Falls (TX) Times Record-News,* recalls that an unemployed geologist once asked him for a job as a reporter. The man didn't have any experience, but James gave him an application, an empty desk, and a typewriter.

"I looked up twenty minutes later, and he hadn't finished the application," James says. "I walked over and said, 'You're welcome to use this typewriter.'"

The man smiled and said, "Well, I don't type."

The moral of the story: there are many ways to get your foot in the door. But once you get inside, prove that you can do the job. You don't have to go to journalism college to do that, but it is a big help.

ARE GOOD GRADES IMPORTANT?

Many editors look carefully at an applicant's grade point average and, these days, even at the entire college transcript for grades in particular courses. Ironically, some admit that if grades were batting averages, they would never have made it to the big leagues.

"I didn't make outstanding grades myself, but it does show dedication and work, an objective," says Don Marsh, editor of *The Charleston (WV) Gazette.*

John Lemmon of *The (Baltimore) Evening Sun* says, "We're not going to hire all people with 3.8 averages and above because there are a lot of other things you want. But if they have a 3.8 average and all the other things are equal, we would probably put them above everyone else."

WARNING: If your grades are below par, do not — we repeat — do not lie about them. As we stated, many editors look at transcripts, not only to double-check the applicant's overall GPA, but to check grades in specific courses. If you lie to an editor about something — anything — you will likely lose any chance of getting the job.

Besides, it's not worth it. Editors look at grades, but they still rank behind good clips, practical experience, and references. Editors realize someone who does well in the classroom will not necessarily do well in the news room.

ARE COLLEGE PLACEMENT OFFICES HELPFUL?

Yes.

Many new graduates get jobs with the help of college placement offices. Some newspapers and communications chains rely heavily on a friendly placement officer in a college journalism department to tip them off to the best and brightest prospects on campus. His opinion is highly valued because he knows the students better than the newspaper's editors and personnel manager.

"They (journalism placement officers) will send their best candidates to us," says Martha Gelhaus, personnel manager of *The Des Moines Register,* owned by Gannett. "They are very helpful."

Don't cheat yourself. Take advantage of their services.

WHAT ABOUT INTERNSHIPS? DO I NEED ONE?

A growing number of editors — particularly at high-circulation papers — are reluctant to hire a new graduate unless he has at least one internship. In the past, college newspaper experience carried tremendous clout. Today, the first question many editors ask is about internships. Intern experience indicates that the applicant has been in a professional news room and has done the job. This is far more important to some editors than clips, which could have been heavily edited. The applicant has a track record and the editor can call the paper where he had the internship and check him out.

Martha Gelhaus of *The Des Moines Register* says her paper will not consider a new graduate who does not have an internship unless "he is an exceptional candidate... We put a lot of emphasis on internships."

You can get a job without an internship. But think of it as a short cut. Ask your college placement office to inquire about internships in your area.

WHERE CAN I WRITE FOR MORE INFORMATION ABOUT INTERNSHIPS AND NEWSPAPER JOBS?

The industry offers some valuable help. For more information about newspaper careers, write for:

• *Journalism Career and Scholarship Guide.* Single copy free. Lists every major college that offers journalism degrees, more than $3 million in scholarships, and general career information and employment prospects. Available from the Dow Jones Newspaper Fund, P.O. Box 300, Princeton, NJ 08543-0800.

• *Newspaper Jobs You Never Thought Of . . . Or Did You?* Up to 50 copies free. Available from the American Newspaper Foundation, The Newspaper Center, Box 17407, Dulles International Airport, Washington, DC 20042.

• *Newspapers . . . Your Future?* Single copy free; $15 per 100. Available from the American Newspaper Publishers Association Foundation, The Newspaper Center, Box 17407, Dulles International Airport, Washington, DC 20041.

• *Suburban Newspaper Careers.* Up to 50 copies free; additional copies $15 per 100. Available from the Suburban Newspapers of America, 111 E. Wacker Drive, Chicago, IL 60601.

• *Careers in News Photography.* Single copy free. Available from National Press Photographers Association, Inc., P.O. Box 1146, Durham, NC 27702.

• *Quill Magazine.* $2 each for "job issue" published every March. Available from *Quill Magazine*, SDJ/SDX, 53 W. Jackson Blvd., Suite 731, Chicago, IL 60604.

WHAT IF I'VE ALREADY GRADUATED FROM COLLEGE AND DON'T HAVE ANY JOURNALISM EXPERIENCE? CAN I GET A JOB?

Yes.

But you have some catching up to do. You are competing against people who have clips, experience, internships, journalism majors, and references. All you have is a burning desire to get into the business.

But that's a good start.

"Nothing done well is done without passion," says Rolfe Neill, publisher of *The Charlotte Observer*, a North Carolina daily with a circulation of more than 200,000.

You really want a newspaper job? You can get one. It may not be *The New York Times*, but you will work.

Bob Richter, a reporter and editor for the *San Antonio Express-News*, remembers when he got bitten by the newspaper bug. He was working in public relations, but shrewdly began playing for the *Express-News* softball team and became good friends with the paper's city editor.

Richter later asked the editor for a job.

"I don't know if you can write, but you're a helluva second baseman," the editor responded. "Come on in. I'll find a place for you."

Okay, it may not be that easy for you, particularly if you have trouble making the double play. But Richter and many others have proven it can be done. And you can do it — if you truly want to. It may be a struggle, but don't give up.

We think the following steps would be helpful if you are considering switching careers and becoming a journalist.

1. **Start writing.** And then write some more. You will have a better chance of impressing an editor if you have something published. Write for the church bulletin, the PTA newsletter, ask the editor of your hometown paper for freelance assignments. Get some clips and put them in an editor's hands. If you have talent, it will show.

2. **Take a journalism course at your local college.** This will give you some experience — and show an editor you are serious about becoming a journalist. Take a night class if you have a full-time job. Take as many classes as possible to learn the basics of reporting, writing, and editing.

3. **Seek an "informational" interview with the editor of your hometown newspaper.** Explain to him that you are not expecting a job offer, but would appreciate some advice. Give him copies of stories you have written and ask for a critique. As we will discuss later, personal contacts are very important. The editor could be a valuable ally when you look for your first job. He may not hire you, but could recommend you to someone else. And if you are lucky, the editor might give you some freelance work.

4. **After getting some clips and experience, start applying for jobs.** Understand that your background may not make you a hot commodity. Chances are slim that you will be hired by a large daily unless you have special talent. Be willing to start at a small daily or weekly. You can do it. Get your foot in the door, start writing, and meet people who can help you move upward.

One last point: you may be nervous about changing jobs. Perhaps you make a good salary. You have a family to support. You wonder whether you have the talent to make it in journalism.

This is your life. This is your decision. But we want to reiterate that you can do it. It may not happen overnight, but you can make your dream come true.

HOW DO I DECIDE WHERE TO WORK?

Everyone has this fantasy of walking out of college and into the news room of *The Washington Post.* A flustered Ben Bradlee, throwing Bob Woodward's story to the ground, runs over and hands you a notebook, a six-figure salary, and a six-month assignment to investigate anything you want.

He was impressed with your clips, Ben explains. He especially liked that analysis you did for the school paper on tuition increases. And that feature on the beer drinking contest, it was boffo.

Glad to have you aboard, Ben says. I don't know what we did without you.

Wouldn't it be great if it was that easy? Wouldn't it be great if we were born with million dollar trust funds?

Someday you may work at *The Washington Post*. But immediately after graduation? Unless you have very, very good credentials, the only way you will break in there is with a grappling hook and explosives after dark.

We are not trying to discourage you. But sit down and honestly assess your ability and background before sending out your resumé. Don't raise your expectations so high that one fall crushes your enthusiasm for the business.

We've seen it happen to dozens and dozens of people. They leave college intoxicated with over-confidence. They expect to be hired by the best. But then a rejection letter comes in and it is taken quite personally. To a disappointed job seeker, it sounds something like this:

"Dear Mr./Ms. One of Thousands:

We have to say we appreciate your interest in our newspaper because our personnel director claims it's a nice thing to do. But we have 13 million applications from people with a lot more experience than you, buddy.

We will put your application on file, which means it will be thrown into the trash can. Should a job opening come up, you are the last person we will contact unless everybody else in the business is killed in a nuclear blast.

Best of luck with your job search, although we really don't care what happens to you."

Try to get a job with a newspaper after graduation — not necessarily a specific newspaper. We cannot emphasize this too strongly. Have ambition and dreams, but don't be concerned if your first choice doesn't have any openings and doesn't expect any in the foreseeable future.

Prove yourself at another paper and your first choice may welcome you with open arms and open wallets. But you will never know if you get discouraged and go into the aluminum siding business after the initial rejection. After all, would you give up dating if your first love told you to drop dead?

"It's a question of being willing to pay the dues," says F. Gilman Spencer, editor and senior vice president of the *New York Daily News.*

Have a heart-to-heart talk with your professors and career counselors before your final year in college. Ask them to compare you to other students. Are you one of the best or do you need help? How about your grades? Are they a clue? Where can you use improvement?

Then quiz as many professional journalists as you can. Based on your experience and clips, do they think you would have a chance of working for their papers? If not, ask them to explain where you fall short. This will let you know what to work on in your final year.

After assessing the comments, ask yourself:

1. **Do I have the experience and clips to land a job at a large metro daily?** You need special talent and some luck to break into a newspaper that has a circulation of more than 200,000. They have very few openings for new graduates. The competition is so fierce that you probably will not be considered unless you have:

   - at least one internship at a respected daily
   - held a high-ranking position at your school paper
   - outstanding references from working editors and your professors
   - excellent clips, which show a variety of skills
   - good, if not outstanding, grades.

   "For instance, to get on *The Philadelphia Inquirer* or *The New York Times,* it's almost impossible," says F. Gilman Spencer of the *New York Daily News.* "You have to be hot, I mean really hot."

2. **Would I be happy working for a smaller paper, particularly in a small town?** This may be a silly question if you live in a small town or have ever lived in one. But if you grew up in a big city, it could be a difficult adjustment and perhaps hinder your development as a journalist. It's hard to keep your mind on work if you're not happy. Conversely, you may have trouble adjusting to a heavily urban area if you are from a small, rural town.

   Assess your personality and decide where you will fit in best. If you easily adjust to new situations, you may develop more rapidly in a new environment because it will be a greater challenge and get your creative juices flowing.

3. **Would relocating be a problem?** Are you married? If so, would your spouse move? Can you move away from your family? Would you have trouble living in a certain region?

   What is more important to you — getting the best job possible or living in a certain area?

   "It really depends on what the person wants to do," says Jay Harris, executive editor of the *Philadelphia Daily News.* "If it's more important to you than anything else to live in California, then apply to California. But you have limited your market. In the best of all possible worlds, you should have no restrictions on where you live. That will increase the options you have to choose from."

4. **Financially, how long can I afford to wait? Do I need a job immediately or can I wait for the best offer?** Money — or the lack of it — can play a major role in determining your future in journalism. It's hard to turn down any job if you are thousands of dollars in debt because of college loans. But remember: a position at any newspaper is better than driving a bread truck.

WHAT ARE THE ADVANTAGES OF STARTING AT A LARGE DAILY?

Money, fame, status . . .

It's true that you can get all three at a 200,000-plus circulation newspaper. But there's something else at a large daily perhaps more important for a young reporter — good editing. Ask any successful journalist why he's made it and he'll tell you about some demanding editor who had the talent and patience to teach him the ropes when he first started. Of course, he might have wanted to strangle him with that rope once or twice. But he became a better journalist.

Some of the most dedicated and competent editors around are working at small dailies. Giving a veteran journalist a bunch of money and dropping him on the city desk of a large metropolitan newspaper will not make him a good editor.

But the laws of supply and demand dictate that large newspapers have the money and resources to hire the best. If you start at a large daily, you are more likely to work under someone who will teach you the right way. This is very important for your career.

"Your first job is the beginning of the longest and most important phase of journalism education," says Jay Harris of the *Philadelphia Daily News*. "You always need to look at a paper that at its best is at least a little bit better than you. Then, your writing will improve and your reporting will improve."

You will work with talented, ambitious individuals from top to bottom at a large daily. It's hard to measure how helpful that can be because good work is contagious. A person tends to work up to — or down to — the level of those around him. It's human nature whether it's a news room or the starting lineup of the Chicago Bears. If your colleagues are breaking stories, you will want to do the same.

WHAT ARE THE DISADVANTAGES OF STARTING AT A LARGE DAILY?

A reporter fresh out of college is sometimes assigned to a beat so obscure he spends half of his time wondering whether the editor remembers his name. He might get published once a week on page B-17 or in the Food section next to a blueberry pie recipe. After a few months, he feels like he has been exiled to Gorki.

Many people say this "lost in the shuffle" feeling prompted former *Washington Post* reporter Janet Cooke to concoct her story about a nine-year-old heroin addict, which won her a Pulitzer Prize and a one-way ticket to infamy. Cooke was assigned to a local zoned weekly edition at the *Post* where many young reporters start. But after several months, she apparently felt the need to do something special to rise above the crowd.

Competition for beats and an editor's attention at a large daily is so fierce that you might have to be adept at office politics to get ahead. Also, you will likely not do a variety of stories or jobs, such as layout, editing, and design. You will cover the city council, or perhaps the health department, for a year. Later in your career, this limited experience could block your path up the ladder.

"If you've already developed your skills, that's fine," says David Lipman, managing editor of the *St. Louis Post-Dispatch*, the 300,000-plus circulation daily. "But only a small number of those who started at that level (metro daily) have really moved ahead in top positions."

WHAT ARE THE ADVANTAGES OF STARTING AT A SMALL DAILY?

Most editors recommend starting at a smaller publication (less than 100,000 circulation) and cite five reasons why:

1. **You will get a better shot at developing your overall skills.** A smaller paper does not have the money to hire a large staff. For example, at a publication with a circulation of 10,000 or less, there may be two or three reporters covering — or we should say trying to cover — the entire readership area. At a paper with a circulation from 20,000 to 60,000 the staff is larger but the workload is the same. You are expected to write two to four stories a day.

   Do this for a few months — if you don't keel over from exhaustion — and you will notice your writing has improved and your questions during interviews are sharper.

   Why?

   Simple. You cannot learn how to be a reporter by reading a textbook. You learn by doing. And at a small paper, you do it until you drop.

   "That's why it's important for a young person . . . to go to a paper where they are just pouring it out on a steady basis," says William Block, president and publisher of the *Pittsburgh Post-Gazette*.

2. **You will cover a variety of beats and subjects.** Work for a small paper for a year or so and you may know how to do nearly every job in the news room. You will cover the city council, business, community issues, and so on. When you apply for your next job, you will have an edge over the competition because you could fit in anywhere.

3. **You will probably participate in the overall operation of the newspaper.** Your editor may ask you to pitch in with editing, layout, design, and story assignment. You can learn all aspects of the newspaper business, which will give you more options later if you want to become an editor or publisher.

4. **You will get more feedback from your editor.** The city editor at a large metro daily may have as many as fifty reporters

on staff. You might talk to him once or twice a day. But at a small paper, you will talk constantly with your editor. After all, there won't be many others in the news room. You will discuss how to write the story, report it, and so on. A good editor can put you on the fast track.

5. **You will be under less pressure.** When a baseball team signs someone out of school, he is rarely brought straight to the major leagues. He is sent to the minors, a more relaxed environment where he is expected to learn. If he makes an error, it will not be analyzed in detail the next day in the media. The manager of the team is more understanding because there is less pressure on him to win.

The atmosphere at a small newspaper is similar. You will make mistakes at your first job unless you are very talented. You might spell a name wrong or forget to check your beat the day a big story breaks. The editor will not be any happier than his counterpart at a large metro. But he will likely be more sympathetic because he has worked with young reporters for years. He expects them to make mistakes.

WHAT ARE THE DISADVANTAGES OF STARTING AT A SMALLER PAPER?

1. **You may get stuck at a bad newspaper.** There are several terrible metro dailies in the country. If you don't believe it, just pick up a few and read them.

Furthermore, the large majority of small circulation newspapers maintain extremely high ethical and journalistic standards because they are run by responsible people.

But, frankly, most bad newspapers are small publications that have become stale over the years for lack of competition. They don't worry about the paper across the street beating them to a story because there isn't a paper across the street, or within thirty miles.

Competition breeds excellence. A lack of competition breeds complacency. You can get lazy if someone isn't looking over your shoulder. So what if you miss a big story? Days after it happens, your paper will still be the first to report it. Your editor may not carefully edit your story because if he makes a mistake, no one may even notice.

Carl E. Beck Jr., editor of the *Spartanburg (SC) Herald-*

Journal (daily circulation 50,000), says he knows a young reporter who's proud of himself because he writes six stories a day and is never edited.

"The copy goes just the way he wrote it . . . That's a terrible newspaper and he's not going to get much out of that experience," says Beck.

A bad newspaper is often run by an editor who either doesn't understand journalism or doesn't care to. He's more interested in knowing the mayor on a first-name basis or perhaps the local car dealer who might lease him a new Lincoln Continental free of charge just because he's the editor of the hometown newspaper.

2. **You will have fewer opportunities to do juicy stories.** You just won't have time. If you're not careful after a year or so, you may wind up with a bunch of ordinary clips that would not impress an editor.

3. **You may develop sloppy habits.** If you are not taught the basics at your first job, you could fall into bad habits that would slow your progress.

4. **Salary.** Small papers don't have much money — for salaries or anything else. They cannot afford to pay a young reporter much more than a living wage. Many newspapers, however, are committed to raising salaries to attract and keep talented people.

WOULD WORKING FOR A WEEKLY NEWSPAPER HURT MY CHANCES OF EVENTUALLY GETTING A JOB WITH A DAILY?

Some daily newspaper editors clash sharply over the merits of starting at a weekly newspaper. Some fear a reporter from a weekly would not meet daily deadlines.

"I think you have a deadline environment that's missing at a weekly," says Robert Giles, executive editor of *The Detroit News*. "An individual would have to be pretty outstanding at one of those publications to get in."

But most editors say if the weekly is good and competitive, the reporter will improve and should be considered as seriously as a candidate from a small daily.

Art Cullen, managing editor of the *Ames (IA) Daily Tribune*, an evening paper with a circulation of more than 10,000, says a weekly is good training because a young reporter will do every job in the news room, from layout to reporting to pasteup.

"That's why I'm in management," says Cullen, crediting his long hours working for an Iowa weekly. "I would much rather hire someone from a weekly. They know what hard work is like."

John Lemmon, managing editor of *The (Baltimore) Evening Sun,* says one of his best reporters started at *The Montgomery County Sentinel,* a Washington, DC area weekly that also was a stepping stone for Bob Woodward of *The Washington Post.*

WHAT ABOUT WORKING FOR A TRADE PUBLICATION OR WRITING PRESS RELEASES FOR A PUBLIC RELATIONS OUTFIT? WOULD THAT BE THE KISS OF DEATH?

A few quotes from the experts:

"If you're going to go into general journalism, go into general journalism and find a way. There are enough papers around," says F. Gilman Spencer, editor of the *New York Daily News.*

"My advice would be to stay away from trade publications. They don't do a thing for me," says Carl E. Beck Jr., editor of the *Spartanburg (SC) Herald-Journal.*

Sounds pretty bleak, doesn't it? But it's not that bad. Many excellent newspaper reporters started at trade publications or public relations companies. But you may have one strike against you. If you want to work for a daily newspaper, you may have to convince a skeptical editor that you have a commitment to newspaper journalism. After knocking down that barrier, show him that you did a good job at the trade publication or the public relations firm.

Chapter 3

Selecting Your Target

SHOULD I SEND MY RESUME TO SCORES OF NEWSPAPERS OR JUST A SELECT FEW?

Send your resumé to scores of newspapers and you may not score. This is not a contest to spread the most paper around the country. You want to convince at least one editor you are a professional, capable young journalist whom he would be happy to hire. Send your clips to every paper in the country and the only person we guarantee you'll make happy is the owner of the local copy machine business.

For some job seekers, it doesn't matter whether they've heard of the papers they've applied to or even the cities in which they are located. William Neubeck, former managing editor of *The Hour* in Norwalk, CT, once received a letter from an applicant who referred to *The Hour* as "The Bridgeport Post and Telegram."

She didn't get the job.

If you can't get the name of the newspaper right, you're going to make a name for yourself — but not the way you want!

We doubt the applicant would have made the mistake if she had sent her materials to only ten or fifteen papers. She would have had time to proofread the letter and catch the error.

Before you protest, we realize it's common for someone who's hungry for that first job — be it as a journalist or janitor — to apply to as many companies as possible. It seems logical. If you apply to 100 different people, somebody must have an opening, right? Or perhaps someone will simply take pity and hire you.

But applying for a job in a news room is different than applying for a job in most other professions. Accuracy is the cornerstone of the business. You must take special care with each resumé, cover letter, and collection of clips. There can be no mistakes, grammatical errors, typos, ink-stained copies of clips, or other embarrassing foibles such as addressing the letter to the wrong newspaper.

But if you mass produce your materials, it is difficult and time consuming to read every piece of paper. So you make mistakes. And, believe us, that matters.

"If there are misspellings, that person is dead," says Carl E. Beck Jr. of the *Spartanburg Herald-Journal.*

Shotgunning your resumés can kill you another way, too. Editors appreciate a highly personalized cover letter that shows a certain writing style and refers to the paper's known characteristics. But that's hard to do when you are mailing out several dozen applications. Editors have been looking at these things for years. They know when they are getting something off an assembly line.

"Jesus, when you just shotgun a bunch of letters from Maine to Florida in the hopes you're going to get a job, I think most editors will resent that," says William Neubeck of the *Asbury Park Press.*

"When I get copied letters, depending on our staffing situation, generally they go into the trash can," says Pic Firmin, executive editor of *The Sun-Herald,* a near 50,000-circulation morning daily in Biloxi, MS.

HOW MANY RESUMES SHOULD I SEND?

It depends largely on where and for whom you want to work. Claude Sitton, vice president and editorial director of *The (Raleigh NC) News and Observer,* recommends sending resumés to your top ten choices. We agree, if you want to stay in your area. You could follow up with telephone calls to each paper and perhaps set up interviews with most of them.

If you are willing to relocate, applications to two or three dozen papers would be okay. But we strongly advise you to only send a resumé to a paper for which you really want to work, and plan to follow up with a telephone call. An editor considers it highly unprofessional — and a waste of his time and yours — to send an application just to be sending one.

So what, you might say. You will likely never work for his paper, anyway, right? True, but you don't burn bridges in this business. You may not want to work for his paper, but later he could be in a position to help or hurt you. What if he leaves his current job and goes to work as the city editor of the newspaper for which it's your heart's desire to work?

An editor has a long memory. So remember: the contacts you make today can pay off later in life.

Another advantage: you will have more time to read and analyze the papers to which you apply. John Carroll, editor of the *Lexington (KY) Herald-Leader*, recalls he once hired a young woman partly because she knew the paper's circulation and its competition.

"That's always flattering," says Carroll.

But it is hard to bone up on the details of 100 newspapers.

We are not trying to limit your options. If you don't get any good leads in a month or so after sending your first batch of resumés, send some more. Just keep the same rules in mind. Take special care with each package.

Of course, we would be remiss if we didn't say that many people got their first jobs after sending resumés to just about every paper in the country. Leslie Lapides, a copy editor for Knight-Ridder's financial news service, cranked out 432 resumés during her final year in college.

"I was desperate because I got interested in journalism pretty late," she recalls. "I didn't have any internships or experience. I thought I'd better try everyone."

After nine months, she accepted an offer from a 30,000-circulation daily in Ohio. But Lapides says she might have landed a better job if she had aimed at a target.

"I've looked back at them (the cover letters and resumés) and they were horrible," she says, laughing. "I can't believe I got anything."

TO WHOM SHOULD I SEND MY RESUME? DOES IT MATTER?

Yes!

Possibly excepting the delivery boy, just about everyone at a newspaper gets a resumé in the mail from time to time. As reporters who have little or no influence over hiring, we've received many applications over the years. A resumé sent to the wrong person will usually be routed to the appropriate editor or personnel officer. But there's no guarantee. A news room can be a highly disorganized place. Don't take chances. It's too easy to get lost in the shuffle — or fall out of the deck entirely.

John Carroll, editor of the *Lexington Herald-Leader*, recalls that his first employer — *The (Baltimore) Sun* —misplaced his resumé and couldn't find him when they wanted to hire him.

"They had no record of who I was," Carroll says. "It took them about a day to get me."

If a newspaper can't find someone it wants to hire, what will happen if you send your resumé to the wrong person?

Do you really want to find out?

Addressing your resumé to the right person will guarantee that it will receive fair and prompt attention. Think about it. When you get a letter addressed to "Occupant," do you give it the same time as a letter addressed to you personally?

Pic Firmin, executive editor of the *Sun-Herald* in Biloxi, MS, says his managing editor — the hiring editor at the paper — will devote less time to a letter addressed to Firmin than one addressed to the managing editor. It's just human nature, Firmin says.

HOW DO I FIND OUT WHO IS THE RIGHT PERSON TO SEND MY RESUME TO?

The average job-seeker looks up the name of the editor-in-chief in the annual *Editor and Publisher Year Book*, which is published every spring, and sends his resumé to him. In fact, a few editors told us that's the surest way to get your application to the right editor, which suggests it's been awhile since they've looked for jobs.

Don't do it.

Why?

First, newspaper editors move more often than Allied Van Lines. That's the business. They go when opportunities arise. Thus, the person listed as the editor in the *Year Book* may be hundreds of miles away working for another paper.

Second, the editor-in-chief or the managing editor listed in the *Year Book* may not be involved in hiring. Every newspaper has a different bureaucracy.

We strongly advise you to call the newspaper before you send your resumé and ask: "Who is responsible for hiring reporters, copy editors, or photographers?" You don't have to identify yourself. Just ask the main switchboard operator or ask for the news room.

SHOULD I SEND MY RESUME TO MORE
THAN ONE PERSON AT A NEWSPAPER?

It should not be necessary if you determine who does the hiring. He will evaluate your application and decide whether to call you in if there is an opening.

But we should not forget just how disorganized a news room can be. Your application could get misplaced even if you send it to the right editor. Or, it may take him weeks, perhaps months, to look at it. Newspaper people have a reputation for being slow when it comes to personnel decisions.

You could send your resumé to the paper's personnel department as well as to the hiring editor.

"Newspapers are not organized and applicants have to recognize that . . . and maybe send their resumés to more than one editor," says John Carroll, editor of the *Lexington Herald-Leader*.

But we advise you do this with extreme caution. We even suggest you approach someone on the paper and ask for advice. Would the hiring editor be upset if you sent your resumé to another editor? You never know. The editor might take it personally.

SHOULD I TAKE THE FIRST JOB OFFERED
TO MAKE SURE I GET MY FOOT IN THE DOOR?

You could get both feet in and never get out.

Try to avoid getting stuck in a dead-end job. After your first year or two, you should be a much better journalist than when you started. But that's hard to do if you work for an inferior publication. So don't blindly take the first thing that's offered, be it a daily newspaper, a weekly or trade publication.

If you are talented, you may get several offers after college. If so, take great care in picking the right place for you.

But for others, it may not be that easy. It may take several weeks or months after college before you get your first offer. Then, you'll ask: if I don't take this job, how do I know I'll get another one? When you are unemployed, any job looks good. Few things in life strip a person of dignity faster than being out of work.

We cannot tell you what to do. You must determine whether you can afford to be out of work any longer or whether you can get a better job later. If you can afford it, we recommend you be cautious. Keep looking until you get the best job possible. You will be glad that you did.

But we understand you can't wait forever. We also cannot overemphasize that you have to know when you have a good offer. Don't sit around waiting for *The New York Times*.

Almost any first job will be helpful, especially if you didn't get any experience in college. Once you get that foot in the door, you can prove yourself and move along. But remember, editors do not consider it a black mark to turn down a job.

HOW CAN I TELL IF A PAPER IS RIGHT FOR ME?

Am I making a mistake?

We ask this before every important decision in life — marriage, having children, buying a home, or choosing a college. We think we're sure about the answer, but we never know until we take the plunge. It's scary because we realize the decision, right or wrong, will mark a turning point in life.

Your first job in journalism can be one of those decisions. You can lay the foundation for a successful career with a job at a good paper. You'll learn skills you can call upon for the rest of your career. But if you get stuck with a bad paper, you may learn bad habits that will haunt you.

Don't be alarmed. A job with a bad paper doesn't have to be a one-way ticket to obscurity. You can still learn, especially if you learned the fundamentals in college.

"It's hard to go wrong when you're sitting down working at a typewriter every day," says N. Christian Anderson, editor of *The Orange County (CA) Register*.

But we emphasize that you should not take just any job.

"If you can afford the luxury, don't get trapped in a job willy-nilly," says William German, executive editor of the *San Francisco Chronicle*. "We've all seen careers go downhill because of that."

Unfortunately, like marriage and other life-changing events, you may not know you made the right choice for several months. You need to be on the job for awhile to know your colleagues and your editors. You'll see if your writing and reporting has improved. You'll find out if there is room for advancement at the paper or if you're getting the experience needed to go to a better paper.

No matter how much research you do, you won't know for sure before working there. However, we think these five tips will help you select the right paper for you:

1. **Read and analyze several editions of the paper.** Then ask yourself:

   - Do reporters get an opportunity to do good stories?
   - Do you think you would improve there?
   - Are stories well edited?
   - How about the paper's coverage? Does it miss a lot of stories or is it on top of things?
   - Would you get a chance to write often?

2. **Ask people in the news room or your professors what they think of the paper.** Do they believe you would do well there?

   Sometimes, you get so close to a situation you need an extra pair of eyes to see what's best.

3. **Ask some reporters on the paper the following questions:**

   - What do they think of their editors?
   - Have their reporting and writing improved since they began to work there?
   - Are they happy? Or, are they looking for other jobs? If so, why?

   You will likely get the most candid evaluation of the paper from its reporters. But be careful. Don't talk to just one person who may be disgruntled. Try to talk to at least two or three reporters.

4. **Get some information on the town where the paper is located.** Decide whether you would be happy living there. Rolfe Neill, president and publisher of *The Charlotte Observer*, suggests you drive around the area "and get some feel for it."

5. **Keep a keen eye during your interview.** You might pick up some clues about the paper.

   What is your impression of the person who interviews you? If he is enthusiastic and asks a lot of questions, that may be a sign you'll get feedback on the job. However, if he comes across as a tub of ignorance, you might have a problem.

   We realize you can't take forever doing an analysis of one newspaper, especially if you are applying to several papers at a time. But if you follow these five steps, it will be well worth the time and investment. Your first experience can be critical.

IS IT WISE TO GRAB A TEMPORARY JOB WITH NO PROMISE OF A LONG TERM POSITION?

Is there a chance of staying on after the job is finished? What about part-time jobs or regular freelance assignments? Are they a waste of time or could they lead to something?

There's no secret to getting hired by a newspaper. Convince an editor you can do the job and will be a good addition to the news room, and you're hired. But it's not that easy if you are on the outside. The editor can look at your clips and check your references, but there still may be doubt in his mind because you are an unknown.

A temporary, part-time, or stringer position can be a great way to get your foot in the door. Once you get inside, you can show they can't do without you.

Sure, if you take a temporary job, there's no guarantee you will stay on when the person you replaced comes back to work. But if it's a good paper, it's worth the risk. You may not get a job this time, but if you did good work you can always come back when they have an opening. You will be a step ahead of the competition because they will know you and your ability.

In addition, there's a good chance your editors will go out of their way to help you find another job. They will likely feel an obligation for bringing you in, although they explained it would be a temporary position.

Freelancers and part-time employees are in a more precarious position. Due to budget problems, newspapers will frequently use freelancers or stringers for a variety of assignments. But in most cases, they do not lead to jobs. If you stay on as a freelancer too long, you run the risk of being taken for granted by the paper.

Talk frequently with your immediate supervisor about landing a full-time job. If he is encouraging, great. But if the news is bad, take the cue and look elsewhere.

Regardless, a regular freelance or part-time position can be an excellent opportunity to get some clips and make contacts and money while you are looking for full-time work.

BEFORE I TAKE MY FIRST JOB, SHOULD I DEVELOP A CAREER GOAL? SHOULD I MAKE SURE MY FIRST JOB WILL HELP ME REACH THAT GOAL?

When you enter the rat race, it's human nature to look ahead to the finish line — your ultimate goal. It may be an assignment as a foreign correspondent or White House beat reporter or perhaps becoming an editor or columnist. Whatever, it is something to shoot for, to fuel your drive to the head of the field during those tough moments in the back of the pack.

We think it's very important to have a goal. Psychologists say if you have one, you will consciously and even subconsciously do what's needed to reach it. But if you do not have a goal, you become stagnant because there's no reason for you to improve. You are happy doing what you're doing.

Indeed, we've seen many reporters so content to have jobs today that they don't think about tomorrow. But after ten years of doing the same thing over and over, this type of person suddenly wakes up one morning and asks: what am I going to do with the rest of my life?

It's sad. Let's say he is thirty-five years old, married, and has children, and suddenly realizes he has not developed the skills necessary to get promoted. He will probably be stuck with the same job for the foreseeable future. Meanwhile, his peers are getting better assignments and salaries. What does he do? Many journalists leave the business, saying they have hit a dead end.

So, we are in favor of goals. But here comes the caution label: if you clearly define your mark of success too soon, it could wind up as a mark against you.

Editors say you need at least one or two years at a paper — to learn the fundamentals and get adjusted to being in the work force — before you can even start thinking about setting a goal.

You've heard of the old saying that a journey of a thousand miles begins with the first step? Well, that's a good lesson for a young journalist; not that we want to compare a successful journalism career with a journey of a thousand miles.

You can have a goal, but take it one step at a time. Make sure you equip yourself with the tools to reach it. Learn how to write, edit, and be a reporter.

"I'm not sure a journalist can really know what his or her

ultimate career goals are until learning the trade, which means getting out on the street and covering a variety of beats for two or three years," says Randall C. Hatch, editor of the *Ogden (UT) Standard-Examiner*.

We know of a reporter who has been in and out of the business now for about ten years, and is forced to compete for entry-level jobs because she still hasn't learned the basics. Inspired by the Watergate investigative team of Bob Woodward and Carl Bernstein in the mid-1970's, she left college ready to be one of the best muckrakers in the nation. But, at this point, she's lucky she doesn't have to rake leaves for a living.

It's a shame. She has talent. In college, she showed good instincts for digging out the behind-the-scenes story. But she was a poor writer, especially on stories which were not banner-headline investigations. She didn't take them seriously because she didn't think she would have to worry about such things when she got a job.

But she became worried after she started applying for jobs. The large metropolitan newspapers rejected her because she didn't have enough experience and lacked writing skills. And the editors of the smaller papers were not interested in a twenty-two year old who wanted to spend six months working on a three-part series on corruption at city hall. At some of these papers, they needed someone who might write three stories a day on city hall. But she was unwilling to do that and, unfortunately, let the editors know it in her interviews. They hired people over her who had less talent, but more desire to improve as all-around journalists.

For a few years, she bounced around from one non-journalism job to the next to pay the rent. She tried to keep sharp by doing some freelance work for local newspapers. But while her colleagues from college were on the inside learning all facets of the business, she was on the outside learning a painful lesson.

She sent another stack of resumés. But editors now questioned why it was taking her so long to get a job. She looked like damaged goods, which she was. Her confidence was shot.

Finally, this would-be muckraker took a job with a trade publication, which was one part reporting and about four parts public relations. She stayed there for a couple of years until she got the itch again to get into newspapers. It was a tough struggle, but she landed a job at a 20,000-circulation daily.

But it didn't work out. Her skills had eroded dramatically. She was fired.

For the past few years, she has gone from one small newspaper to the next looking desperately for her niche.

What did she do wrong?

Wanting to be a top-notch investigative reporter is fine. But there's more to journalism than spending your time researching records and meeting sources in dark alleys. For starters, you have to learn to write. You can have a great story, but you must tell it in words. People won't read it if they can't understand it. You also must learn how to work a beat. Some of your best stories will come from casual talks with your daily contacts.

Unfortunately, she put the cart in front of the horse. If she had taken the time to develop her overall skills, she probably would have become a highly sought after investigative reporter. As it is, however, she has to search for a new job every two years or so.

We are not trying to scare you. But we've seen many others who are so concerned about the future, they fail to learn NOW!

"Everyone has a career goal," says Don Marsh, editor of *The Charleston (WV) Gazette*. "But life takes funny bounces. You can't be cold blooded."

We advise you work at your first job as if it were your last, and not just some stepping stone to bigger and better things. If you don't take your job seriously, it's going to show and it will be more difficult to get the second job you want. You will not cover the White House if you don't learn how to be a reporter.

For example, Bill Moyers, the award-winning commentator for CBS-TV and the Public Broadcasting System, started as a reporter for the *Marshall News Messenger*, a small daily in east Texas. And Dan Rather, the anchorman of the CBS Evening News, began his career at *The Huntsville Item*, which was then a small weekly in Texas.

A goal is important, but it should be a finish line and not an obstacle.

Editors also say a young person in any field should be flexible. You never know when opportunity will come calling.

"When I first got out of college, I thought I wanted to be a reporter. Five years later, I wanted to be an editor," says Joel Kramer, executive editor of the *Minneapolis Star and Tribune*.

Chapter 4

Loading Your Weapon

WHY IS A PERFECT RESUME PACKAGE SO IMPORTANT?

"Dear Ms. Ogden," the letter begins. "I am writing you because I am very interesting in obtaining a reporting position with the *Lawrence Eagle Tribune*."

Problem is, Ms. Ogden was not the managing editor of the Lawrence paper. She was the managing editor of *The Middlesex (MA) News*, a daily based in Framingham, about an hour's drive south of Lawrence.

That's not the way to bowl over an editor who considers accuracy a vital trait in a reporter.

Strangely, the writer, a young woman one week out of college, correctly typed Victoria Ogden's name, title, and newspaper only a few lines above. If the applicant had just proofread her letter, she might have caught the mistake.

To compound her sin, the letter was pockmarked with erasures, typos, and white-outs. She typed letters over letters and took no pains to disguise the fact. And she was even wrong about the name of the *"Eagle Tribune"* — there's a hyphen in it! Though earnest, ambitious, and quite possibly intelligent, the applicant sent a loud message that she is sloppy and inaccurate.

She didn't get the job.

You can study hard in college, spend long hours working for the school newspaper, and have all the ambition and desire an editor could ask for. You can have experience as an intern and good references.

But if you can't get your message across in the resumé package, you will have a tough time beating out the competition and landing an interview. And if you can't get through that door, you can't get a job. The resumé package — a cover letter, a resumé, and a half dozen clips of stories — is an early, make-or-break part of getting a newspaper job.

In many cases, the package is your first contact with the editor for whom you want to work. First impressions are always important in a job hunt. In journalism, they are crucial. Editors must separate the wheat from the chaff, and they don't often go back for a second look.

You might think editors could ignore such petty details as typos or misspelled words. After all, shouldn't your track record and talent be more important than neatness? Can't an experienced editor shrewdly rub off the cloudy veneer of a bad resumé to reveal the shining jewel of the journalist inside?

Real life doesn't work that way.

"Journalism is a business of precision," says N. Christian Anderson, editor of the *The Orange County (CA) Register*. "If you don't have that in your cover letter or resumé, then forget it."

Put yourself in an editor's visor. Top notch reporters make editors look very good. And you can't afford to hire too many flops if you want to keep feeding your kids and paying the mortgage. So you look for prospects who have something special going for them. You look for sparkling writing. You look for applicants willing to work a little harder than the rest of the crowd. You look for young men and women who are on the ball, who can sense the importance of doing things right — such as writing a good, solid cover letter or a nice, clean resumé.

"Usually, it's the end of the day (when an editor reviews resumés)," says Jay Harris, executive editor of the *Philadelphia Daily News*. "You're in no mood for half-hearted efforts."

What will he think of an applicant who sends a bleary, photocopied resumé marred by misspelled words and handwritten additions? Or one who sends a load of stale clips? Given his sixty-hour work week, should he waste his time interviewing some guy who doesn't take the trouble to spell his name correctly on the cover letter? How lazy and inept would the applicant be on the job if he screws up his first contact with you?

Bad applications go in the trash or wind up in dusty file cabinets somewhere, entombed forever.

Stay out of that tomb. You want your resumé and clips staring up from the top of an editor's desk — or at least filed in his mind for ready reference.

It's not as hard as it sounds. Just remember to check for mistakes. Then go back and check again. And again. And play up your strengths. Stand out from the crowd.

WHAT SHOULD I PUT IN A RESUME PACKAGE?

There are three parts: the clips, the resumé, and the cover letter explaining what you want. We'll take a look at each of these, then view real letters and resumés to see how NOT to get a job in journalism.

WHAT MAKES A GOOD COVER LETTER?

There's no simple answer. Editors themselves disagree about what kind of letter they like. A letter that begins, "Lois Lane, move over," may grab one editor's attention and thoroughly disgust another.

A cover letter is an art, not an exact science. Still, there are some steps you can take to put you ahead of the competition.

But first, some background.

A cover letter is a one-page letter, written in proper business form, that accompanies your resumé and clips. You use it to introduce yourself to an editor and state what you want: a job and an interview. You also use it to flesh out your resumé and play up your strengths. Be crisp and brief.

Newspaper editors put greater emphasis on cover letters than employers in most fields. Cover letters require a deft writing touch, brevity, and clarity — skills a good reporter or editor needs.

"The better a cover letter is, the more attention it (the resumé package) will get," says Carl E. Beck Jr., executive editor of the *Spartanburg (SC) Herald-Journal.*

"The letter says . . . whether the individual is just shopping around or whether he really has thought about your newspaper," says Robert Giles, executive editor of *The Detroit News,* which has a circulation of nearly 700,000.

It's bad — possibly fatal — to send a resumé without a cover letter. It would say you have not made the effort to find out how the real world works. Always top your resumé with a cover letter.

If you write well, a cover letter gives you an extra opportunity to stand out from the crowd. Writing a first-rate letter is a tough task. You've got to trumpet your abilities without overblowing them. And demonstrate some understanding about the newspaper without sounding pompous.

No, it's not the easiest writing project in the world. But take some time with it and show it to friends before sending it. Many editors use the cover letter to weed out candidates.

WHAT ARE SOME OF THE BASICS OF A GOOD COVER LETTER?

Type and individually sign every cover letter you send. Even if you are writing similar versions of your cover letter to several newspapers, don't send something that appears to be mass-produced.

Never, repeat never, try to dodge work by typing the editor's name on carbon copies or photocopies of your cover letter. Editors hate that. They think if you are too slothful to make this effort to land the job you want, how are you going to perform day after day on the beat?

For the same reason, don't use a dot-matrix computer printout for a cover letter. Some editors might not mind, but it's best to be on the safe side. Type your cover letter on good, clean paper. Create the impression you are thoughtful, careful, professional, and flawless. Don't give the editor an excuse to throw your package in the trash.

Get a good typewriter. If the insides of letters like "o" and "a" are clogged with ink, clean them out. If you make a mistake in your letter, don't smear "white-out" over it or use an eraser. Start over. Appearances count.

William Neubeck, an editor with the *Asbury Park Press* in New Jersey, recalls that when he was growing up his parents forced him, "to the point of tears," to write college application letters five or six times until he got them right. People who don't show Neubeck the same courtesy don't get very far.

HOW CAN I OUTSHINE THE COMPETITION?

Do some fairly painless research.

By now, you have probably talked with friends and professors about where you'd like to work. To find out more, consult the *Editor and Publisher Year Book,* which gives key facts about newspapers, such as addresses, telephone numbers, paid circulation figures, frequency of publication, and the names of people in the top positions. It will tell you whether the paper is part of a chain or locally owned, information you should know before applying. The *Year Book,* available in the reference department of most public libraries, will give you a sense of any newspaper in any region of the country where you'd like to get a job. Take a pen and note pad with you and jot down the names and other data. Be sure to get the proper spelling.

Get some copies of the paper. You can call its circulation desk and ask for a mail subscription or inquire about getting some back issues. Sometimes you can tell from a few editions whether you even want to work at that paper. All papers, especially small dailies, make mistakes from time to time. But if the paper's front page is consistently cluttered with spelling errors and murky, dull stories, this may not be the place for you.

It sounds like a lot of trouble, but it's worth it. Your analysis will require only the few minutes it takes to read a paper and jot down some notes, but it will help you write a good cover letter and give you the background to sound sharp when you sit down for an interview. You'll feel more confident and do a better job.

HOW ABOUT AN EXAMPLE OF A PERFECT COVER LETTER?

Unfortunately, it wouldn't be very helpful if we printed a model of the perfect cover letter here because (a) editors themselves disagree about what makes a great cover letter, and (b) editors would start receiving letters copied straight out of this book — and slavish imitation does not win jobs in this business. William Handy, managing editor of *The Wichita (KS) Eagle-Beacon,* for instance, says he's impressed with an applicant who can "craft a cover letter that shows a real understanding of the issues, that hasn't been taken from a 'How to Write a Resumé' guide."

But you won't go wrong if you give your cover letter some thought. Remember, show an editor you have special skills and talents that could help make his paper better. Make that editor want to turn to your resumé and give you serious consideration.

DO ATTENTION-GRABBING STUNTS REALLY WORK?

Jim Naughton, associate managing editor at *The Philadelphia Inquirer,* has a slew of stories about the shrewd stunts applicants have pulled at his paper. Naughton, who once wore a chicken head mask to a press conference, once received a package of top-rate clips, a resumé, and a photo of the applicant — wearing a chicken suit. Another person sent him an in-depth, eight-page investigative piece — on Naughton himself. Still another sent him a huge pair of shoes, adding a note: "Just wanted to let you know the shoe size I can fill."

Did those stunts work? Well, they certainly grabbed the editor's attention, but that isn't enough. Naughton was more impressed by great clips and a good reputation in the business. Other editors agree. No one expects you to be a circus clown or an advertising executive to get a newspaper job.

"One person printed a magazine with resumé and job letter," recalls David Lipman, managing editor at the *St. Louis Post-Dispatch.* "It was a well-done magazine, just delightful to look at. But when it was all done, we were looking at the clips and they were not as dramatic as the resumé and the job application. We thought, 'Boy, is he cute and clever. Why doesn't he go to work for an advertising firm?'"

You can overdo the salesmanship. After all, good journalists spend their lives trying to cut through the bull — and they can smell it a mile away.

William Neubeck, an editor at the *Asbury Park Press,* says an applicant once sent a colleague a four-page bound resumé which on the cover had a picture of himself standing on the steps of the state capital looking at the dome.

Avoid slinging that stuff. Try to be confident without being pompous.

Another no-no: trying to get overly familiar with an editor.

One eight-year veteran of Texas newspapers wrote to Jim Craig, then Washington bureau chief for the Texas-based Harte-Hanks Newspapers.

"Dear Mr. Craig," she wrote.

That was a perfectly suitable way to address the bureau chief, but then she crossed it out and hand wrote "Jim," although she had never met the man. She may have been trying to show Craig she was one of his peers, but she sounded foolish in implying a familiarity that didn't exist. And she was not on an equal footing. She was seeking a job. Keep that professional distance.

Some applicants make the mistake of getting "cute" in their cover letters, writing about the weather or going off on a bender about their quest for personal enlightenment.

Another letter to Craig, this one a computer printout, reads: "I sit before my amber pc screen wondering how to begin. What tidbit of my personal history will make you curious about me and my story."

An editor is not interested in the emotional turmoil you experience writing a cover letter. He doesn't care what color your "pc" (presumably personal computer) screen is. He is probably more curious about why you did not realize the second sentence of your letter should end with a question mark.

"But wait. There are twists and turns in the story that might interest you," the applicant writes. Craig was not exactly breathless with anticipation.

Just get to the point. Pretentious writing is not the way to a good editor's heart.

Your best bet: be lively, but straightforward and professional. Again, keep the focus on your special strengths: experience, education, and background. Be sure to stress how each of those could work for you at that particular paper. Experience is usually the most vital factor in an editor's eyes. Stress that one above all others and sell yourself.

One job applicant writing to Victoria Ogden, then managing editor at *The Middlesex (MA) News,* had the right idea with this fairly punchy lead: "You've probably been hearing from hordes of fresh college graduates with little experience looking for a spot on your staff. I'm not one of them."

That makes an editor turn to the resumé to see if the applicant can back up her claim. This applicant shrewdly cited her work on the student paper and her experience covering town meetings, conducting interviews, and generating stories on her own. That experience looks good to the editor of a medium-sized daily in New England.

The applicant also stated clearly in her letter what she wanted: a full-time job as a reporter. And she said she would call Ogden within a week to inquire about an appointment at the editor's "earliest convenience." While her letter was not outrageously eye-popping, it touched all the bases in a professional manner and got the editor's attention.

"I look for a cover letter that says implicitly: I'm worth your time . . . If the first two graphs are interesting, I'm likely to read the third," says Jay Harris, executive editor of the *Philadelphia Daily News*.

WHAT SHOULD A RESUME INCLUDE?

Everything an editor needs to tell him you're worth interviewing.

Resumé is a French word meaning "summary." A resumé sums up your work experience, training, and background. It is the core of the package. An editor uses it to size up where you've been, what you've been doing, and how well you've been doing it.

But a resumé is not as cut and dried as you might think. Even though it takes the form of an objective list of your life — and it should be scrupulously accurate if you don't want to blow your chances — you must shape it to play up your strengths and ignore the negatives.

Put the most interesting and important information at the very top. Less pertinent information — the stuff you don't want to play up as much — goes lower down.

Though a resumé can be two or three pages long, it is a good idea to keep it as short as possible — one page, if you can. Applicants with vast experience in journalism might be able to legitimately fill three pages with dazzling accomplishments of real interest to an editor. But applicants should avoid padding their resumé with extraneous material simply to make it seem more impressive. Most editors will not be taken in by length. They are more likely to take an interest in applicants who understand the value of brevity and clarity. The idea is to give an editor a thumbnail sketch of your background and accomplishments — without making him do any trimming.

Your resumé must be well organized and pleasing to the eye. It should be typed perfectly. If it's out of date, don't cross over sections and hand write additional information. Start over. Never send a carbon copy to an editor, but a photocopied resumé is okay, as long as the machine makes a bright, neat copy on good, white paper. If the copy leaves gray streaks or blobs of black on your resumé, find another one that works better.

As with the cover letter, make sure there are no typed-out letters, erasures, or white-outs. You are selling a product — yourself. Don't forget that packaging sells products.

Some people pay to have their resumés typeset and printed. That might be a good idea if you're just starting and plan to send resumés to a number of papers. But it's not necessary. Editors are not looking for absolute beauty. They want to know you care about what you are doing.

What do editors check for in resumés?

Education, experience, and some sign that the applicant is committed to the business. They also will check out information and applicants have been known to lose jobs because they lied on a resumé. If you have great clips and seem professional in an interview, they will be more likely to overlook the fact that you didn't have a 3.8 grade point average than to forgive you for lying that you did.

A resumé is divided into several parts. Let's take a look at them:

YOUR NAME AND ADDRESS

Your name should be at the very top of the page, usually centered. A couple of lines below should be your address (including zip code) and a telephone number or numbers. Make it as easy as possible for an editor to reach you. Some people list their name in the upper left-hand corner with their address and phone number in the upper right-hand corner. Either way is okay. Just give the resumé a balanced, pleasing appearance.

JOB OBJECTIVE

State the job you want: starting reporter, copy editor, sports editor. Be specific. Don't write, "I'll do anything," even if you will. You can talk about that in the job interview.

"Starting reporter" says you are willing to start on the bottom but you want a reporter's job, as opposed to some lesser position such as an editorial assistant.

EXPERIENCE

List your employment in reverse chronological order. Your most recent writing experience should be at the top. This section should be devoted to news experience. If you worked the past three weeks as a short-order cook, but worked last summer as an intern at a newspaper, play up the newspaper experience and list the short-order cook job under an "Other Employment" section.

List your starting and leaving dates, your title, and the exact name of the newspaper, magazine, or other news outfit you worked for. Briefly, describe what you did using third-person: i.e., "covered breaking police news, wrote feature stories about crime in Mayberry, filled in on desk during summer, did some editing and layout."

If you have absolutely no news experience, decide whether your education or job experience would look better to an editor. If education, place that section of the resumé higher than experience. (We remind you it will be extremely difficult to get a newspaper job without some experience, so start right away to get some — a stringer's job or writing for a weekly publication will get your feet wet.) But no matter what your level of experience, you should analyze how it can help you get the job.

Some editors look first at education. If you had great grades at a great school, play that up.

"If I see an Ivy or a Reed or a Swarthmore . . . and I see good clips, I might get especially interested," says F. Gilman Spencer, editor and senior vice president of the *New York Daily News*, a tabloid with circulation of more than 1.2 million.

List your college experience at the top of the education section. Include the dates you started and finished, the college name and location, your degree, your major and minor. If you had outstanding grades, list your class standing, any honors you received, and your grade point average. For someone with years of experience, those details are less important and can even clutter up a resumé. But if you've been in school within the past few years and did a great job there, put it in. It gives an editor at least a sense of how hard-working you were. On the other hand, if you spent all your time working part-time jobs at the local newspaper and got lousy grades, don't mention the grades at all and play up the experience. Keep it positive at all times. Think about what will impress the editor.

Also list some extracurricular activities (although you should list your college newspaper work with the job experience section).

Remember, editors look for experience you could put to use on the job. So this portion of the resumé could do you some good. If you took a number of science and biology courses, mention it. That can help you during a job interview. Everybody has experiences that can help them somewhere along the line in journalism. Search for yours, mull them over, and be prepared to talk briefly about them during the interview.

Hatch of the *Ogden (UT) Standard-Examiner* says he's impressed by an applicant who "has a unique educational background or experience. For example, a journalist who has a law degree or an applicant who is an unusually good cook, etc. The added training helps a journalist bring greater depth to his articles — and greatly improves his ability to report on a complete subject if he has a good foundation in that field." Mention that experience — briefly — in your resumé.

PERSONAL DATA

Include the date and place you were born, your marital status, your health (if excellent), and your hobbies. You might wonder why an editor needs all this information. He really doesn't, but editors are by nature snoopy, that is, interested in people. A little bit of personal information makes you seem a more rounded, more interesting person to him. Give him something besides life and death issues to chat about at the job interview. If you both turn out to be baseball fans or cooking enthusiasts, for example, that might help break the ice.

"Resumés today have far too little in them," says Claude Sitton, editor of *The (Raleigh, NC) News and Observer*. "I want to be able to take a resumé and see the person's background . . . I'd rather have too much than too little."

One word of caution: Don't pretend to be something you're not — say a chess expert or an outstanding fisherman. Editors sometimes will grill you on your hobbies to see how honest you are.

REFERENCES

The standard wisdom says don't include references with resumés. But many editors say they want them. So put them in. Make it easy for editors to find out how good you are. Think of past employers who were impressed with your work and barring that, a professor or faculty adviser who is willing to give you a plug.

There are many basic forms for a resumé. But here are two standard versions:

CLARK KENT
16 Lois Lane
Metropolis, USA 43256
(312) 555-5555

JOB OBJECTIVE

Political Reporter

WORK EXPERIENCE

MAY 1979 to PRESENT --

City reporter for The Daily Planet, an afternoon daily which has a circulation of 300,000.

BEAT: Crime. Politics. Superman

ACCOMPLISHMENTS: Won first prize in national SDX contest for two-part series called, "Superman, Superguy." Second-place award for spot news story on Batman's retirement. Honorable mention for three-part series called, "Robin: Will He Ever Live Up To His Potential?"

EDUCATION

Graduated May 1979 with journalism degree from the University of Smallville. Minor, agriculture science. Staff reporter for The Husker, the campus newspaper. 4.00 G.P.A.

DATE OF BIRTH

Smallville, USA, May 8, 1955

HOBBIES

Reading. Volunteer work. Flying

REFERENCES

Perry White, editor of The Daily Planet. (312) 555-5543.
James Olsen, managing editor of The Daily Planet (312) 555-4109.

JOHN SMITH
65 Main Street
Anytown, USA 43256
(713) 555-5555

JOB OBJECTIVE: Starting Reporter

EXPERIENCE:

1987-1988 (senior year)   Staff reporter and copy
                                 editor at The Call, a daily
                                 campus newspaper. Involved in
                                 overall production of the paper.

1986-1987 (junior year)   Campus correspondent for The
                                 Big City Daily Bugle. Averaged
                                 one story a week.

1985-1986 (sophomore year)   Staff reporter for WASD, a
                                 campus radio station.

1984-1985 (freshman year)   Editor of The Dream, a campus
                                 literary magazine.

EDUCATION: Graduated from Thomas Jefferson
                                 University in May 1988 with
                                 journalism degree. Minor,
                                 biology. 3.20 G.P.A.

AWARDS AND HONORS: President of Biology Club.

DATE OF BIRTH: April 25, 1966, Anytown, USA

HOBBIES: Skydiving. Poetry. Bowling.

REFERENCES: Marty Janes, editor of The
                                 Big City Daily Bugle.
                                 (713) 555-1000

                                 Dr. Paul Jones, dean of Thomas
                                 Jefferson University college of
                                 journalism.
                                 (713) 555-4000

SHOULD I SEND CLIPS?

Your resumé package is not complete without a half dozen clippings of your best stories — clips, in the lingo of the profession.

You don't need to send actual clips, but send at least high quality photocopies. Resist the temptation to send a fat pile of stories. The more you send, the more editors are likely to give each one a cursory glance. They don't have time to pore over a dozen clips.

"Don't send me a four-pound package," says Rolfe Neill of *The Charlotte Observer*.

Keep that in mind. Editors are not bowled over by bulk. The simple fact you've had stories published will not impress them. They are interested in quality. A total of six is about right.

Try to choose a mix of stories — hard news, features, and above all, investigative pieces. Editors are more likely to be interested in well-rounded reporters, applicants who can turn out both lively hard news stories and bright features. Avoid sending a series of stories that are slight variations on the same theme.

When going over your clips, keep that editor in mind. Unless you are applying for a job at a paper in the same town where you broke a great local story, avoid sending him clips which have a strictly local interest.

"An editor once told me that if someone was on a train from New York to Washington and they stopped in Wilmington and picked up a paper, the stories he would read are the stories that are interesting, compelling, where you don't have to know the characters," says Jay Harris, executive editor of the *Philadelphia Daily News*.

That's a valuable tip. As you go through your stories, think about which ones might be read by that visitor picking up the paper. Make sure the hard news stories in your package — through gripping detail, terrific quotes, and the drama of the event — do not rest on foreknowledge of the people and places in them. You may have gotten a great front page with a story about a county commissioners' meeting, but if the story means little to people who do not know the personalities and issues involved, you would be wise to look for something else.

Don't go out of your way to find stories you wrote in a "literary" style. Editors are far more likely to take notice of stories the average reader would enjoy, ones about interesting people and events told in simple language.

Editors say they look for clarity, brevity, and pacing in stories. They size up the way the writer organized the information. Did the reporter get to the heart of the story? Did he or she go out of their way to find and report telling details?

Surprisingly, not all editors are impressed by great clips. They do not know if an applicant's stories have been heavily edited. Nevertheless, clips are often the one item in the resumé package that will persuade an editor to give you his time for an interview. Choose your clips always with that reader in mind. Give the editor something fun to read.

"If an editor who's busy is sitting there and enjoying what he's reading, then you've gone a long way," says Jay Harris of the *Philadelphia Daily News*.

HOW CAN I GET AN EDITOR TO REALLY READ MY PACKAGE?

If you have contacts who can pave the way for you with that editor, use them. If you have a friend who works for the paper, see if he would mention to the editor that your resumé is coming. If you have a relative or college professor who knows the editor, have him place a friendly call. You can have all the talent in the world, but unless an editor notices you, you won't get the job.

WHAT TYPES OF MISTAKES CAN TRIP ME UP?

Everybody makes mistakes. And it's hard to know — when you are fresh out of college — how to go about getting a job. But this is one time you have to be perfect. We're going to show you some mistakes made by applicants in actual letters and resumés sent to *The Hour*, a 21,000-circulation daily in Norwalk, CT. We've blotted out the names and other personal information of applicants to protect their identities. If you can avoid these common gaffes, you will be far ahead of the game.

Dear Mr. Neubeck:

Five years ago, having left college because there was nothing there I wanted, pining away in a ratty apartment in downtown ███████████ I desperately begged god for a deal. I told him if he would just help me write something I could sell, I'd give the money to the church. I was sure I could become a writer if I just got started somehow. Well, I got started eventually, and success didn't just come happily ever after, but being a writer is an old dream, so I've kept chasing it.

I earned my bread and butter during college by working with my brother in his used-car business. I started out washing, polishing and repairing cars, then began supervising and became vice-president of ███████████ Motors, Inc., but I worked much harder when I joined my school paper than I ever did in the car business. Statesman has usually been 16-24 pages during the last few years, roughly double what it used to be (the pages are 59 picas wide and 15 inches high.) The squabbling and infighting in the student government, which once dominated the front page of the paper, has been pushed back to make room for more important things. I took this even further when I became news director, because I discovered, leafing through The Chronicle of Higher Education, that there was a lot going on in government that our readers would be interested in, but never hear about otherwise. The immigration reform bill congress is working on right now, for example, includes a clause requiring that most foreign students leave the U.S. after receiving their degrees.

As I said, I never worked as hard worked as vice-president of ███████████ Motors as I did putting out Statesman. Twelve-hour days were common, and didn't seem that strenuous. I wouldn't want to continue going without sleep as often as I did in school, but I know hard work doesn't hurt if you enjoy what you're doing. I enjoyed my work at the ███████████ Herald also, because even though it was a lot more fun being an editor at Statesman, I'm anxious to work in situations where people teach me, not the other way around.

I thrive on pressure, concentrating best on slightly hectic days, and am familiar with using VDT's. I am available for an interview nearly anytime.

Sincerely,

EXAMPLE A

EXAMPLE A

This letter violates at least three cardinal rules of cover letters:

1. Individually type and sign every letter.
2. Use proper business form.
3. Get to the point.

This fellow used a mimeographed letter on blue paper and typed Neubeck's name at the top in letters that are plainly lighter and different from the body of the text. Not exactly the way to show the editor you want to work for his paper.

Neubeck calls the letter "one of these beauties where he's written this long letter telling me his life story, all xeroxed and then he just puts 'Dear Mr. Neubeck' at the top of it. And, of course, no inside address or anything like that. That's ridiculous."

Proper business form requires your return address in the upper right-hand corner and, to the far left just below that, the name of the editor, his title, the newspaper, and its address. The worst sins, though, are the letter's rambling introduction and its unseemly personal tone.

And "God" is capitalized, by the way.

CT 06770

Sept. 20, ████

Mr. John P. Reilly
Executive Editor
The Hour
346 Main Avenue
P.O. Box 790
Norwalk, CT 06852

Dear Mr. Reilly,

I believe my vast experience in a newsroom can be an asset to your
newspaper. Presently, I work full-time for a small newspaper in
Naugatuck and am looking for a part or full-time position in your
editorial department.

I enjoy being a reporter and I am a very good hard news and feature
writer, am organized and a hard worker.

Enclosed is my resume for your inspection. I believe I possess the
qualifications necessary for your consideration and am available for
interviews at your convenience.

Thank you for your time. I look forward to meeting you and discussing
the details of a position with the newspaper.

Sincerely,

EXAMPLE B

EXAMPLE B

Here, the applicant uses proper business form, but she turns the editor off by grossly overstating her qualifications. Play up your strengths, but don't inflate them. One year with a small paper in Naugatuck, CT does not qualify as "vast experience in a newsroom."

This applicant would have fared better by leaving out the word "vast" and by citing specifically how her experience would make her a valued employee at *The Hour*.

June 9, 1984

John Reilly, editor
The Hour
346 Main Ave.
Norwalk, CT 06852

Outrageous!

Dear Mr. Reilly:

Please allow me to commend you on the fine paper you produce.

Although I work as a general assignment reporter for a ▓▓▓▓ ▓▓▓▓ newspaper in northwest Indiana, I plan to relocate soon.

After reading The Hour, I would consider myself fortunate if you would review my resume.

The Hour particularly impressed me with its Financial/Business section, Hour Neighbors feature and Where They're Working and Home/Town People columns. Your local news coverage says you have the same kind of commitment to the community there that I feel toward the residents of the towns I cover here.

The editors here say I have the ability to organize and synthesize information and to reach the reader on a personal level. Given the opportunity, I would make a substantial contribution to your staff.

Since it would be purely coincidental for you to have a position available at this time, I would appreciate if you would keep my resume on file and consider me in the event of an opening. In the meantime, may I send you a sample of my work?

I plan to be in the Norwalk area during the week of July 9. If it would be convenient for you, may I stop by your office to see your operation and to introduce myself?

I will call the week of June 25 to confirm an appointment. Thank you for your consideration.

Sincerely,

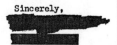

EXAMPLE C

EXAMPLE C

Here's what Neubeck says about that opening line: "Now, that's presumptuous on the part of a young writer applying to me for a job, telling me that this person should commend me on the paper I write, especially since she comes from Indiana and obviously doesn't read *The Hour* regularly. Now, that's just outrageous."

That may sound a bit harsh, but Neubeck has a point. You don't want to appear to be passing judgment on a paper or overly buttering up the editor.

This applicant was trying. She bothered to get copies of the paper, read, and study them in detail. That's impressive. But she could have put that edge to better use. She says what she likes about the paper, but does not say how her own experience and talents would enhance the paper. While her letter is generally written in a professional manner and her closing paragraph shows good sense, she spends too much time describing the paper and not enough time selling her own skills. Remember, anyone can compliment an editor. You have to show why the editor should hire YOU.

Don't lecture editor if they don't respond you don't want to work there anyway!

June 26, _____ 21217

William Neubeck, Editor
The Norwalk Hour
346 Main Avenue
Norwalk, CT 06851

Dear Mr. Neubeck:

I don't understand. In fact, I am <u>utterly</u> confused. I've sent
you two resumes since April. Here it is June 26th and I've yet
to receive a reply. Shame on you, Mr. Neubeck! I thought you
were a professional journalist.

Another resume? Yes. Enclosed is <u>another</u> resume. Take a look.
You might be impressed. Meanwhile, I will be waiting for your
response.

                        Persistently Yours,

EXAMPLE D

EXAMPLE D

Proper business form, but grossly improper behavior. This gets an editor's attention, all right, but insulting him is not the right way to do it.

"You're applying for a job with me and . . . you're lecturing me before you even come to work?" Neubeck says.

Neubeck explains that he has no secretary and cannot answer every application. Usually, he gives the least attention to letters from distant states.

Bergenfield, N.J. 07621
December 8, 1981

Mr. William Neubeck
Editor
Norwalk Hour
Norwalk, Connecticut
06851

Dear Mr. Neubeck,

I am writing in response to your ad for a copy editor that I read in Editor and Publisher.

Presently I'm an editor with The Shopper Newspapers and News Beacon, in ████████ I edit copy, lay-out pages, assign stories, take pictures and cover stories when necessary.

My prior news experience includes working on the copy desk of The ██████ News, in ██████████, editing stories and doing the "News at a Glance" page.

Following my graduation from college, I worked as a broadcast reporter for radio station ████ in ██████████, N.Y. As a reporter I covered the usual range of local news; city government, state and county legislature, the courts, boards of education, sports, public affairs and features. Specifically, I worked on the Lakeland teacher's strike, the longest strike in New York history, the prison guards; strike, the recall of the Dutchess County sheriff, and the Serge Motti murder trial. I also covered the Lake Placid Olympics in 1980, doing a series of interviews with the then unknown U.S. Hockey Team.

I also have continued my education, pursuing my Master's Degree in Public Communications at ██████ University when time and money permit.

I hope you accept this letter as an application for a position on the Norwalk Hour. I will be in contact with you soon, and I hope at that time we can schedule an interview.

EXAMPLE E

EXAMPLE E

This applicant, seeking a copy editor's job, uses "presently" when he means "currently" and he misspells "lay out." There's no hyphen. Not a great recommendation for a copy editor, whose job it is to catch mistakes.

Brooklyn, New York 11210
April 6,

Mr. William Nuebeck
Managing Editor
The Hour
346 Main Avenue
Norwalk, Connecticut 06851

Dear Mr. Nuebeck:

"He knows everything. He is aware not only of what goes on in the world today, but his brain is a repository of the accumulated wisdom of the ages."

--Editor Stanley Walker on reporters.

Whenever it's pointed out that reporters always seem so rushed, I can only think it's because we're all desperately trying to meet these impossible, but necessary, standards. As for myself, I still haven't absorbed the accumulated wisdom of the ages, but my experience as an editor and a reporter has only bolstered my determination to make general assignment reporting for a daily newspaper my career.

As you can see on the enclosed resume, much of my experience has been under the title of editor. Through my editorial duties, I've gained an understanding of the entire newspaper production process, as well as layout and design.

However, I should point out that I consider myself a reporter first. I'm fully aware of the personal sacrifice required for reporting, having dedicated myself to the job a long time ago. I've experienced the endless leg-work, the time pressure, the frequent dead ends and the countless hours of phone work. I've come to expect long, hard hours with low pay.

I'm also experienced at finding stories and judging newsworthiness. As you can see by the enclosed articles, my writing covers a broad range of styles: news features, straight news, news analyses and profiles. All the enclosed articles I found myself, as is the case with most of my articles.

I hope I can fill the role of general assignment reporter for your paper. I'd be happy to meet with you and discuss the possibility of my working for The Hour. Please contact me about a time and place convenient for you and I'll be there.

Sincerely yours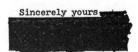

EXAMPLE F

EXAMPLE F

"I'm not a fan of the cute or tricky lead to get a job," Neubeck says. "Here's somebody quoting from Stanley Walker on reporters in the beginning. I don't like that kind of lead and I automatically turn those people off."

The moral: Don't be cute. Get to the point.

To make matters worse, this applicant commits the ultimate sin of spelling the editor's name wrong. A good journalist must spell names correctly.

Nashua, N.H. 03063

The Norwalk Hour
346 Main Ave.
Norwalk, Conn. 06852

Mr. Reilly:

Being a non-skier in a snow-bound state can have its
drawbacks. So, when the Farmer's Almanac--and a host
of other weather authorities--began predicting a very
snowy and cold winter, I began thinking New Hampshire
isn't quite the state to be living in.

I thought last winter--and spring--was bad, but apparently
I haven't seen nothing yet. And I hope I don't see it.

What I'm looking for is another job, preferably in
southern Connecticut, before the first or second
snow flies.

I'm in the Norwalk area often and would like to stop by
to talk about any job openings you may have at the
Hour.

Looking forward to talking with you.

Sincerely,

EXAMPLE G

EXAMPLE G

An editor doesn't want to hear you'd like to work for his
paper because the weather's better down there.

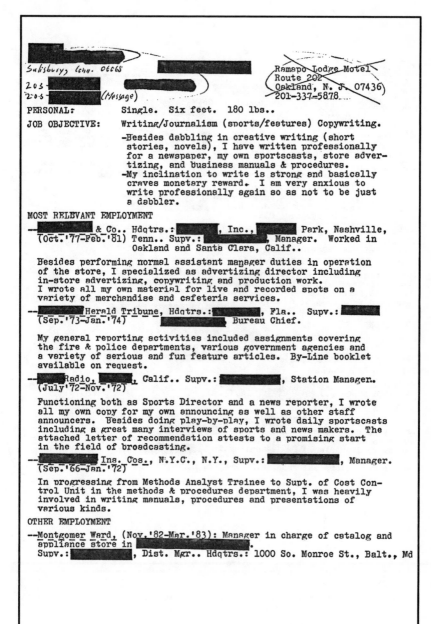

Salisbury, Tenn. 06665

203-
205-   (Message)

Ramapo Lodge Motel
Route 202
Oakland, N. J. 07436)
201-337-5878

PERSONAL: Single. Six feet. 180 lbs..

JOB OBJECTIVE: Writing/Journalism (sports/features) Copywriting.

-Besides dabbling in creative writing (short
stories, novels), I have written professionally
for a newspaper, my own sportscasts, store advertizing, and business manuals & procedures.
-My inclination to write is strong and basically
craves monetary reward. I am very anxious to
write professionally again so as not to be just
a dabbler.

MOST RELEVANT EMPLOYMENT

--▮▮▮▮ & Co.. Hdqtrs.:▮▮▮▮, Inc.,▮▮▮▮ Park, Nashville,
(Oct.'77-Feb.'81) Tenn.. Supv.:▮▮▮▮, Manager. Worked in
        Oakland and Santa Clara, Calif..

Besides performing normal assistant manager duties in operation
of the store, I specialized as advertizing director including
in-store advertizing, copywriting and production work.
I wrote all my own material for live and recorded spots on a
variety of merchandise and cafeteria services.

--▮▮▮▮ Herald Tribune, Hdqtrs.:▮▮▮▮, Fla.. Supv.:▮▮▮▮
(Sep.'73-Jan.'74)▮▮▮▮ Bureau Chief.

My general reporting activities included assignments covering
the fire & police departments, various government agencies and
a variety of serious and fun feature articles. By-Line booklet
available on request.

--▮▮▮▮ Radio,▮▮▮▮, Calif.. Supv.:▮▮▮▮, Station Manager.
(July'72-Nov.'72)

Functioning both as Sports Director and a news reporter, I wrote
all my own copy for my own announcing as well as other staff
announcers. Besides doing play-by-play, I wrote daily sportscasts
including a great many interviews of sports and news makers. The
attached letter of recommendation attests to a promising start
in the field of broadcasting.

--▮▮▮▮ Ins. Cos., N.Y.C., N.Y., Supv.:▮▮▮▮, Manager.
(Sep.'66-Jan.'72)

In progressing from Methods Analyst Trainee to Supt. of Cost Control Unit in the methods & procedures department, I was heavily
involved in writing manuals, procedures and presentations of
various kinds.

OTHER EMPLOYMENT

--Montgomer Ward, (Nov.'82-Mar.'83): Manager in charge of catalog and
appliance store in▮▮▮▮.
Supv.:▮▮▮▮, Dist. Mgr.. Hdqtrs.: 1000 So. Monroe St., Balt., Md

EXAMPLE H

-2-

-- ████████ Management, Inc.(Jan.'82-Aug.'82): Building Manager in
Charge of the operation of four buildings. Supv.: ████████.
Hdqtrs.: 141 Main St., ████████..

-- ████████ Stores, (Apr.'81-Nov.'81): Co-Manager assisting manager
in operation of variety store. Supv.: ████████, Dist. Supv..
Hdqtrs.: ████ So. Park Victoria Dr., Milpitas, Ca.

-- ████'s Toys, Hobbies & Stationery, (Sep.'76-Sep.'77): Asst. Mananager
assisting manager in operation of variety store. Supv.: ████████,
Mgr. Hdqtrs.: Merchants West, L.A..

-- ████ Family Discount Stores, (Oct.'74-Apr.'76) : Manager supervising
operation of discount department store. Supv.: ████████, Dist. Mgr..
Hdqtrs.: Opa Locka, Fla..

--Kentucky Fried Chicken, (Apr.'74-Aug.'74): Asst. Manager helping to
operate fast food restaurant. Supv.: ████████,.Dist. Manager.
Hdqtrs.: Ft. Lauderdale, Fla..

-- ████████, (Apr.'73-Aug.'73): Claims Adjustor processing
varied small claims. Supv.: ████████, Sr. Claims Adjustor.
Hdqtrs.: Ft. Myers, Fla..

MILITARY SERVICE (Jan. '63-June '63)

-Following graduation from Naval Officer Candidate School at Newport, R.I.:
 --Served from 9/63 to 6/65 on ████████ (ocean going minesweeper) as
 Minewarfare Officer/1st Lt.. Homeport: Charleston, S.C..
 --Served from 6/65 to 6/66 as Asst. Flight Support Officer at VT-2,
 U.S. Naval Aux. Air Station, ████████..

EDUCATION

B.A. from ████████ University (████████)-1962.
--Political Science major. Psychology minor.
Graduate of ████████ High School, ████████, N.Y. (1958)

PERSONAL BACKGROUND

**Born.............████████, New Jersey.
**Raised & Educ....████████, N.Y..

PREVIOUS EXPERIENCE

-Day camp counselor, ████████, N.Y..
-Maintenance worker, public schools, ████████, N.Y..
-Door to door salesman, advertizing, Seattle, Washington.
-Asst. to librarian, ████████ University, ████N.Y..
-Waiter, cook's helper, at college fraternity.
-Department store salesman, R.H. Macy's, Garden City, N.Y..

*** *** *** *** *** *** ***

EXAMPLE H

The resumé is a mess. If you can't do better than cross out the name of the motel you lived in and handwrite a new address, you're not going to get far. Retype your resumé if you make changes. And organize it better than this so the editor can find his way around.

NOTE: "Montgomer Ward." It's Montgomery Ward.

OBJECTIVE   Responsible position with opportunity for advancement.

QUALIFICATIONS   Objective Writer   Eager Learner   Enjoy close contact with
                   Tactful Communicator   Self Starter   artists, scientists,
                   Goal Setter   Team Worker   researchers, professional
                   Likes Special Projects Adept Interviewer   personnel.

ACHIEVEMENTS   Wrote and completed 19-page investigative reporting piece well
                   before deadline.

                   Conducted a difficult interview and interpreted numerous observations
                   into a sensitive, professional article.

                   Kept an imaginative journal of my recent travels to California
                   and Hawaii.

                   Wrote 100-page fiction story at age 13.

                   Developed a consumer response chart with little direction.

EDUCATION   B.S. Journalism/Communication – University of ▮▮▮▮▮▮

EXPERIENCE   Dr. ▮▮▮▮▮▮▮, Chiropractor – Managed two-woman office.
                   Developed x-rays, assisted doctor with treatments. Motivated
                   patients, developed knowledge of chiropractic method.
                   Hartford Insurance Group – Assisted unit in administering insurance
                   products and trained new employees.
                   Gloria Stevens Figure Salons – Counseled and supervised members.
                   Increased salon efficiency, improved camaraderie, generated
                   enthusiasm, exhibited dependability, completed studies in advanced
                   anatomy and nutrition.
                   New Haven Register – Wrote news and features. Established rapport
                   with government sources and issue knowledge.
                   FINAST Supermarkets – Analyzed and charted consumer complaints,
                   helped develop Consumer Affairs Department. Supervised operations
                   in director's absence.
                   Van Law's of Suffield – Assisted managers in special event
                   coordination, travel and sales strategy, trained new employees.
                   Olsten Services – (Since 1975) – Demonstrated and cultivated
                   ability in all office procedures while on temporary assignments
                   for diverse area businesses.

PERSONAL   Excellent health, willing to travel.
                   Have my own independent business.

EXAMPLE I

EXAMPLE I

Check out these "qualifications." This tells the editor that you are a hype artist.

William Neubeck
Managing Editor
The Hour
346 Main Ave.
Norwalk, CT 06851

at present, now or currently.

Dear Mr. Neubeck,

I am presently the city reporter for the ▮▮▮▮▮▮▮ ▮▮▮▮▮▮▮▮▮▮ and I would like to be considered for any openings you might have for a general assignment reporter, staff reporter or sportswriter.

My experience in journalism has consisted of one year working for the ▮▮▮▮▮▮▮▮▮▮▮, a city-wide daily newspaper serving all of ▮▮▮▮. From August, 1982 until December, 1982, I was a police beat and general assignment reporter doing spot news and feature stories. From January, 1983 until the time of my graduation, I worked for the ▮▮▮▮▮▮▮ as a sportswriter and sports copy editor. My beats as sportswriter were women's gymnastics, high school golf and tennis and Stephens College athletics. I also spent one year working as a sportswriter for the Eagle, a campus newspaper at the American University in Washington, D.C.

Following my graduation from the University of Missouri-Columbia School of Journalism, I spent six weeks as a general assignment reporter and photographer for the ▮▮▮▮▮▮▮▮ News-Journal before joining the ▮▮▮▮▮▮▮▮ in September, 1983. I enjoy the position but would like to move on to a larger newspaper closer to home.

If a job is available or becomes available, please get in touch with me at the address listed below. I am enclosing my resume to aid in your decision.

Sincerely

, MO 65340

EXAMPLE J

EXAMPLE J

This applicant uses improper business letter form. He also uses "presently" when he means at present, now, or currently. That may sound picky, but journalism is a business of precision. Be perfect when you make that first contact.

William Neubeck
Managing Editor
The Hour
346 Main St.
Norwalk, CT 06851

Is he kidding?

January 2, 1985

Dear Mr. Neubeck:

Having completed my undergraduate studies in journalism here at Bowling Green State University, I am now in the process of finding a suitable position at a daily newspaper.

Having heard many of my professors speak highly of The Hour, I wrote to your circulation department recently and requested several copies of your paper.

After reading and reviewing them carefully I was quite impressed with the way The Hour covers Norwalk and the surrounding area.

My goal as a graduating senior is to find a position on a high quality publication. The Hour, Mr. Neubeck, would be an excellent opportunity.

I have a great deal of experience for a college student, having interned on a daily in New York City, worked for over a year with the Toledo and Columbus bureaus of the Associated Press, and held almost every position my college paper has to offer.

I have enclosed a copy of my resume and several clips for your perusal. I think you will see that I have all the makings of a good, solid newspaper reporter.

Mr. Neubeck, I would very much like to discuss with you any current or future positions there might be for me at The Hour. I will be in Connecticut next week and will call your office to inquire about an interview.

Thank you for your time and I hope to see you soon.

Sincerely,

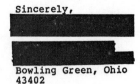

Bowling Green, Ohio
43402

EXAMPLE K

EXAMPLE K

Another case of buttering up the editor.

February 27, 1984

Hour Publishing Co.
346 Main Avenue
Norwalk, CT 06851

ATTN: John P. Reilly

Dear Mr. Reilly:

As a free-lance journalist who has written for both daily and weekly publications
and wire services in Massachusetts, New York and Vermont, I would like to apply to a
Connecticut daily such as The Bridgeport Post and Telegram.

Please accept this letter and resume as an introduction and application to you
for a position as staff reporter or writer in your news department.

My published artilces have informed readers of such local issues as teen-age suicide,
the media's role in politics and refuse-to-energy management.

I would be very happy to show you some of my clips at your convenience. I will
call you at the beginning of March and will look forward to your response.

Yours sincerely,

Briarcliff Manor, NY 10510

Enclosure

EXAMPLE L

EXAMPLE L

"Well, if you're going to apply to *The Bridgeport Post* and *The Telegram,* apply to them," Neubeck says. "Don't apply to me."

Also note misspelling of "articles" in the third paragraph.

February 19th,

Dear Mr. Neubeck,

I am writing to apply for a job as a reporter with the <u>Hour</u>. I will graduate from yale in May of this year and hope to start work this summer.

Most of my extra-curricular time since high school has been devoted to journalism, in particular with the <u>Yale Daily News</u>. My job as features editor there ended in October of last year, whnn we elected a new managing board. But I have kept reporting throughout this academic year for my jobs as stringer for <u>Newsweek</u> and for the UPI.

My internship this past summer in ▮▮▮▮▮▮ convinced me that I do want to pursue journalism as a career. And I would very much like to start in Norwalk.

I have taken the liberty to enclose some clips and a resume with this letter. I hope this will be enough material for you to consider my application for a job. Of course, I would be delighted to come see you in Norwalk whenever you like.

I look forward to hearing from you soon.

Sincerely,

EXAMPLE M

EXAMPLE M

Can you tell what's wrong with this letter? You got it — everything!

Improper form. Lousy typewriter. Typos and type overs. This applicant says she went to "Yale" but she doesn't seem to realize the school's name is capitalized. "Taken the liberty" is right out of Monty Python's Flying Circus. It's pompous.

And, to top it off, she signs the paper with a scribble. Nothing else. She doesn't have her name typed under the signature, which is standard practice. She doesn't type her address above, either.

Who is this mystery applicant? Is a busy editor going to take the time to find out?

▇▇▇▇▇▇ Smith College
Northampton, Mass.
01063

No handwritten letter!
we type in our business
April 14, ▇▇▇

The Norwalk Hour
346 Main St.
Norwalk, CT.

Dear Sir or Madam,

I am a second year student at Smith College in Northampton Mass., majoring in English Language and Literature. At the present-time I am seeking summer employment in the field of journalism.

I would prefer (of course!) a position as an intern or aide on the Hour, however, I am well aware that these jobs are quite scarce. Do you have anything available? Are there positions for clerk/typists — I type 45 wpm. and am experienced with the IBM-PC word processing programs.

I am hard working and energetic. I would do whatever might be assigned to me (I was a chambermaid). I hope that you will consider me in your summer employment plans.

Thank you,

▇▇▇▇▇▇▇▇

EXAMPLE N

EXAMPLE N

"I mean, we've moved a little ways since Ben Franklin. We work with typewriters and computers."

NOTE: Neubeck since became an editor at the *Asbury Park Press* in New Jersey.

HOW SHOULD I ASSEMBLE MY PACKAGE?

Neatness counts. Make it easy on an editor to find his way through your material. It might be a good idea to assemble the cover letter, resumé, and clips in a folder with a clear plastic cover. Mail the package in a large, sturdy envelope. Editors do not appreciate tearing open business-sized envelopes stuffed full of clips that flutter to the floor.

We know of one reporter who beat out another qualified candidate for a job because her clips were neatly copied onto standard-sized paper and placed lovingly in a clear plastic folder. Her competition glued his clips onto construction paper, leaving some of the columns hanging over the edge of the page. The editor opted for plastic. "We thought she'd be better organized," he later said.

Chapter 5

The Battle, Or How Do I Get My Foot In the Door?

HOW IMPORTANT IS THE JOB INTERVIEW?

Get an interview and anything could happen. Fail to make that personal contact, and you won't get a job — not unless you won last year's Pulitzer Prize, and maybe not even then.

Some job placement experts say the interview is almost all that matters in the job search. Everything else — the resumés, cover letters, telephone calls, and background research — is not as important as the first impression you make when you shake that editor's hand.

The way an editor feels about you in person can put you in contention, even if your clips, experience, and education leave something to be desired. Many editors tell us they have been unimpressed with a beginning journalist's clips and resumé, but the applicant turned it around in an interview and edged out more "qualified" competitors to win the job.

"We've had cases where they didn't really look like the hottest prospect on paper, but we were just impressed and went ahead and hired them," says Asa Cole, general manager for Massachusetts weeklies owned by the Harte-Hanks newspaper chain.

Personal contact can make all the difference in the world. Experienced reporters have seen the phenomenon dozens of times. A source gives you a chilly reception over the telephone, but sit down with him, attach a face to your voice and the hostility and reticence often melt away. It works the same way with editors, who are human beings, too.

Be more than a name on a piece of paper and faceless

voice over the telephone. Get an interview at every one of the papers you've targeted.

Once you look an editor squarely in the eye, you have a crucial edge over every other candidate who was not persistent enough to get that far.

SHOULD I TRY TO GET AN INTERVIEW AT A PAPER WHERE THEY SAY THERE ARE NO JOBS?

Absolutely.

The papers you've targeted may not have jobs available, but don't let that deter you. Turnover at newspapers, particularly dailies with a circulation of 75,000 or less, is high. By the time you have your interview, there may well be a spot open. And if not, there may be one six weeks later.

You've got nothing to lose — aside from some time and relaxation — and everything to gain.

WHAT CAN I GAIN FROM THE INTERVIEW?

1. **You can impress an editor so much he will keep you in mind when the next job opens up.** Suddenly, your resumé will have meaning to an editor and go into the "active" pile.

   "If someone has been down and done well on the test I've had him take, he would have a hot chance for the job," says Don Marsh, editor of *The Charleston Gazette.*

2. **You will make a contact, which may pay off later in your career.** "Say you end up working at a paper that's not quite as strong as you want, but you make a contact (at a better paper). Then you can follow up with a letter saying, 'I took this job, but here's a few clippings. At some point, I'll get my chance to work at your paper,'" says John Carroll, editor of the *Lexington (KY) Herald-Leader.*

3. **You can learn a lot about journalism and the job hunt by sitting down with an editor who knows his way around the news room.** Editors are often flattered to be asked for advice and more than willing to give some pointers.

   "Talk to people like me," says F. Gilman Spencer of the *New York Daily News.* "I can juice 'em up pretty good."

4. **You can do some sizing up yourself.** How sharp is this editor?

Is he committed to journalism? Does the news room have decent equipment? Are the editors unbearably obnoxious or rude?

One beginning journalist we'll call Cynthia had an interview at a small daily. During her visit, she saw an editor interrupt a reporter who was in the midst of a telephone interview, typing quotes at a computer terminal. The impatient editor grabbed the phone, hung up on the source without saying a word, and issued new orders to the reporter. Cynthia weighed that behavior in her decision to take another job.

5. **It's good job hunting experience.** Even if nothing pans out, you've had a dry run. At the next interview, you will be more relaxed and in command. You'll know what to expect and have had time to bone up on questions you flubbed during the first interview.

6. **You never know what may turn up.** An editor is often good friends with editors at other papers in the region. If the editor has absolutely nothing available but takes a real shine to you, he might try to steer you to another paper. Sometimes, he will even give you a plug. Spencer of the *New York Daily News* has often played that role. Though he does not have nearly enough job openings to accommodate the talented young reporters who come to him, he has recommended some of them to the top newspapers in the country.

Contacts are the name of the game in any job hunt. Strike up a conversation during the job search and make as many friends as you can when you land a job. And don't burn any bridges behind you. You may turn around to see your enemy standing on the same side of the river, blocking your path. Journalists jump from paper to paper.

"Build as many of those contacts as you can. You never know in three years where you're going to be, or where a person you know is going to be," says Mark Nelson, a reporter for *The Dallas Morning News*, which has a circulation of nearly 400,000. "It's a small world in this business."

WILL MY RESUME GET ME AN INTERVIEW?

Sometimes, yes. Often, no.

Even a terrific resumé package may go unnoticed. That's where the magic word — persistence — comes in.

If you've taken our advice, you've already done a lot of hard work, asking friends and professors for information about papers, delving into the *Editor and Publisher Year Book*, reading newspapers, assembling clips, writing and proofreading cover letters. You might feel like taking a short breather, and waiting for the editor to return your serve.

Bad idea. Remember, stand out from the crowd. Hopefully, you've moved up by making your resumé package lively and letter perfect, but now it's time to take the next step.

One to two weeks after mailing the package, call the editor and ask:

- whether he received your material
- how soon you can come in for an interview — at the editor's convenience, of course.

"He probably will have gotten them (your clips and resumé) but it's good to make sure . . . and it shows a little bit of interest," says Tom Squitieri, Washington correspondent for the *Boston Herald*.

William Garland, Washington correspondent for Harte-Hanks Newspapers' Texas papers, says you should make your first call within a week.

"Don't let your resumé sit in a stack with ninety other resumés. You've got to stand out," says Garland.

We know you'll have some jitters about making that first call. That's natural. But take a deep breath and go ahead. And keep plugging until you get a straight answer from an editor. Just remember, you will make tougher calls than this one as a reporter. That's the business you're in.

You'd be surprised how many applicants — including journalists with years of experience — don't bother to make that call. They may expect the editor to take one look at their credentials and leap to the nearest phone. That's not real life. For one thing, an editor is not all-knowing. He might not see just how good you would be for his paper. For another, the typical editor has more chores than can be done in an eight, twelve, or sixteen hour day. When you're putting out a daily paper, the task of sifting through job applications ranks near the bottom on the priority list. A stack of paper doesn't talk back on deadline.

By making that call, you find out where you stand and what your next step will be. You also add some flesh to the bones of your resumé. You draw closer to the editor; no longer a piece of paper, you're now a real person with a real voice at the other end of the telephone line. Best of all, you demonstrate to an editor that you are a person who takes initiative and is serious about landing a job. And you put some distance between yourself and all those lesser candidates who don't have the gumption or brains to call.

"If I get a letter saying they'll call me in two weeks, I take them at their word. Okay, call me," says William Neubeck. "But the overwhelming majority don't call back."

Marc Stern, a reporter with Copley News Service, recalls trying to land an interview with an editor at *The San Diego Union*.

"I was just relentless. I called him all week and he always managed to slither off the hook. Finally, on a Friday he said he didn't have time because he had to go to an editors' conference in Palm Springs. So I drove off to Palm Springs and greeted him when he got to the hotel."

Stern didn't get the job, but he did get a chance to sit down and talk newspapers with the editor.

"That's the kind of aggressiveness you need," he says.

TIME OUT FOR A WARNING: Catch an editor at the most convenient time possible for him. If you reach him just before deadline, your admirable trait of persistence turns into something else: a pain in the butt. Put that editor in a good and relaxed mood. Then, he is more likely to cut you a break.

So if you have an acquaintance who works for the paper, find out what time of day the editor isn't tied up on the desk or in meetings.

Some job placement experts suggest avoiding Monday calls because most people return to work after the weekend grumpy and tired; they tend to give you short shrift.

Also, try to reach the editor who does the hiring. You should already have obtained his name and addressed your resumé package to him. Don't hound the executive editor if it's the managing editor you should be talking to.

One last word of warning. If you're fresh out of college with no experience, don't badger some editor from a big metropolitan daily if he's trying to be nice and make it clear you're not ready yet. There's no need to overdo it; editors can recommend you to friends at smaller dailies. But if you hound the living daylights out of him when you're clearly in over your head, you can lose some genuine help.

Always call, but keep your ears open for signals from the editor. Don't try to smash through a brick wall. But you might want to give a wooden one a shot.

HOW CAN I KEEP AN EDITOR FROM PUTTING ME OFF?

When making that call, keep two words in mind: FIRM and POLITE.

Psychologists say the person on the receiving end of a phone call is always at a disadvantage. Use that. Take the initiative. Ask the editor to meet with you as soon as possible. Stress you would be available whenever it would be convenient for him. Ask if you might stop in next week some time.

Go with the flow. If the editor says he could sit down with you at such and such a time, grab it and politely thank him.

If the editor hems and haws and says he's really not doing much hiring, kick it into a higher gear. Say you understand how busy editors are, but you wouldn't take much time and would really appreciate the chance to present yourself. Say you understand there aren't many positions, but you enjoy reading his newspaper and feel you could make a real contribution if a job ever did open up. If the editor still plays the "you'd be wasting your time" line, ask if he could then sit down for a few minutes to give you some pointers on job-hunting. (That could lead to a job referral.)

If the editor says, "Call me next week," do that. And keep calling until an interview opens up. Be FIRM and POLITE. Not cocky. Not arrogant. Be respectful of an editor and his time, but make it clear you aren't a wallflower.

Do you risk becoming a pest?

"Of course, but you've got to do it," says Andrew Barnes, editor and president of the *St. Petersburg (FL) Times*.

Sure, you will sound like a jerk if you push too hard for an interview at a paper that's clearly out of your league. On the other hand, shrinking violets don't beat out the competition. Pests sometimes do.

"A little chutzpa doesn't hurt," says William Block, publisher of the *Pittsburgh Post-Gazette*.

One way to counteract the negative effects of persistence is to be POLITE while you're being FIRM. A hiring editor will judge whether you're the kind of person he wants representing his paper. Persistence is a terrific calling card for a reporter. Obnoxious and inappropriate behavior is not.

WHAT IF PERSISTENCE FAILS?

Call in any other contacts you have. Ask a professor (preferably one with recent news room experience) to make a call on your behalf. Search your brain for anyone else who might help: influential relatives, acquaintances who are big advertisers, friends in other departments at the paper. Don't insist on making it on your own at this point. There will be plenty of time for that later.

"Anyone who might throw a block for you," says William German, executive editor of the *San Francisco Chronicle.* "I've seen people who I would not (otherwise) see because they have come to my attention because the assistant circulation manager has friends."

WHAT IF I'M TIGHT FOR FUNDS? WILL THE PAPER PAY MY WAY TO AN INTERVIEW?

Unless you've got some impressive experience and you are applying to a metropolitan daily, probably not. Again, welcome to the world of professional journalism. Unlike big oil companies or Wall Street investment firms, daily newspapers don't usually shell out big dollars to recruit and fly in talent.

If you're looking for a job near home or college, no problem. Otherwise, it might be a good time to take that cross-country drive you've always dreamed about.

"There's a greater chance of being interviewed if you're making the trip at your own expense," says Joel Kramer of the *Minneapolis Star and Tribune.* "What I would recommend to someone after college is: if you get any glimmer of encouragement from a few papers around the country, pack up your old car and make a trip around and just do it on vacation."

The applicant who seizes the initiative and says he will be available at the editor's convenience has a big advantage over the applicant who sits at home waiting for an editor to send an airplane ticket.

William Garland of Harte-Hanks Newspapers, who loved Santa Fe and wanted to work for the city's Gannett-owned daily,

The New Mexican, decided to try his luck on the road. One week after sending his resumé, Garland drove 350 miles to Santa Fe from his hometown of Perryton, Texas. He was working in Perryton as news editor of his local paper, a job he got one month after graduation.

Garland stopped at a phone booth and called *The New Mexican's* city editor, John Bott, to ask for an interview.

"It was obvious he was impressed I was there and had a strong enough interest in the city to come over and try my luck," Garland recalls.

While Bott confessed he didn't have a job to offer Garland then, he told him he would keep him in mind. When Bott left the paper several months later, he left a note behind — keep Garland in mind if a spot opens up.

Garland was later hired.

By making personal contact and following up on his resumé, Garland stood out from the crowd.

SHOULD I VISIT AN EDITOR IN PERSON WITHOUT CALLING AHEAD?

Only as a last resort. Some applicants have landed jobs doing that. But generally, it's lousy business practice and a bad idea. You could end up cutting your own throat.

"Good Lord, that shows a profound lack of courtesy and consideration for my time," says William Neubeck, an editor at the *Asbury Park Press.*

That says it all. Unless you are desperate to land a job at that paper and have exploited every other avenue, it's better to use polite but firm persistence to get an interview. Even if you are passing through town, it's a good idea to call ahead before you drop in on an editor.

HOW SHOULD I PREPARE FOR AN INTERVIEW?

No matter how talented you are, preparation can be the difference between landing a job and getting lumped with the also-rans.

A newspaper job interview is no mystery. It's a predictable event. That means you can plan ahead to say and do the right things at the right time to appear head and shoulders above the competition. And there's nothing tricky or deceitful about it. By following our plan, you're simply showing an editor you are thorough and hardworking.

The first thing: a job interview is not what it seems. You are not there to sit back and answer factual questions about yourself posed by an editor. You shouldn't go in "cold," expecting your experience and talent to carry the day.

To be successful, drop the passive stance and play an active role. Sell yourself. Convince the editor you're better than the competition and exactly the type of person — intelligent, outgoing, and hardworking — who will represent the paper well.

You will need some basic psychology and some inside knowledge of the newspaper to do that. Work out some of your answers ahead of time so you don't appear to be stumbling. Once you've done your homework, your nerves should be jumping a little bit less and your self-confidence should be soaring.

If you clear out some of the fear and clutter in your brain ahead of time, you should have no problem relating to that world around you.

Your first task is to do some research on the paper. The best and easiest way is to read the thing — every day for two to three weeks, if possible. As you read it, jot down some notes. List the things you really like about it. Analyze the ways you could fit in. Note the subjects the paper tends to cover. If it's a suburban paper in a growing market, does it focus on problems of growth, such as pollution, traffic, or crime? Is any single sector of the economy — say, agriculture, oil, or high technology — vital to the region's well-being? Would any classes you took in school help you cover those issues?

Memorize a few observations on your list. During your interview, pop some of them into your conversation. Tell an editor how you can help the paper do an even better job than it does now. Remember to talk about what you admire in the paper — flattery can help if it's not overdone.

Also, know the answers to these questions before walking into an interview:

- What's the paper's circulation?
- How many editions does it publish?
- Who's the paper's competition?
- How fierce is that competition?
- Who owns the paper? Is it owned by a chain or a family?

- Has it won any Pulitzer Prizes or other major awards recently?

Some of this information is in the *Editor and Publisher Year Book,* but see if your journalism professor knows anything. Call a reporter in the news room, and get him chatting about the paper. Think about ways to put a positive spin on the various things you've learned about the paper and drop them into your interview.

Another good idea is to develop some local story suggestions to spring on an editor.

Tom Squitieri, the former Washington correspondent for *The Sun* in Lowell, MA, knew when he applied for that job that Lowell was the first great mill city in America, and was in the midst of a remarkable economic revival. When he met with the editors of the paper, he noted that it did not run Lowell-specific employment figures when the government released them every month. He said he would file stories each month on the morning the figures were released, which would help the paper tell "the Lowell success story."

"I had about four or five story ideas and I think that helped a lot," he says. "(An editor) wants someone out there who can recognize what a story is and go out and get the story and bring it back."

Is all this preparation worth the hassle? Every editor we interviewed for this book emphasized how impressed they are with an applicant who demonstrates some knowledge of the paper.

Every editor.

William Handy, managing editor of *The Wichita (KS) Eagle-Beacon,* says the worst thing an applicant can do is make it "obvious that they haven't read the newspaper very well."

HOW SHOULD I DRESS FOR AN INTERVIEW?

Your clothes should tell an editor you are solid, serious, mature, and professional. You won't always dress that way on the job, perhaps, but you should for that crucial interview.

Psychologists say an employer often makes up his mind about an applicant in the first thirty seconds of an interview. Blow that first impression and you'll be struggling to get out of a deep hole for the rest of the session — and you'll probably never make it back to the top.

Gruff, seasoned editors may claim to see past the trappings to the real person underneath, but they're subject to the same subconscious manipulation as everyone else. A well-dressed, well-groomed applicant seems more intelligent, mature, and able than his sloppier counterpart. An applicant wearing a yellow checkered suit with a soup-stained purple tie appears younger, less intelligent, less stable, and not as well prepared to handle the challenges of the job.

Editors size up each applicant who walks through the door as a potential representative of the paper. If your fly is open or your pantyhose are run, the editor will form a frozen mental picture of you appearing in front of the public that way – and that's not the image he wants the paper to have, to say the least.

"It's rare that a really sharp person would show up not being concerned about the way they appear," says Dick Tarpley, retired editor of the *Abilene (TX) Reporter-News*.

"You don't want to hire any hippies," says Don James, editor of the *Wichita Falls Times Record-News* in Texas. "You don't have to hire a guy who doesn't comb his hair."

William Neubeck of the *Asbury Park Press* adds that he has had enough of reporters "covering the City Council looking like they should be going to a Bob Dylan concert."

So, men: wear a dark suit and a striped tie that picks up the colors of your suit. Wear a white cotton shirt, professionally pressed if possible. Better not wear a vest; you don't want editors thinking you're too spiffy to do the grubby job of reporting. A suit jacket with a good pair of dress slacks will do, but a suit is better. Avoid garish colors. Shine your shoes. Black is preferred. Get a haircut before the interview. Don't wear overpowering aftershave.

Look slightly better and crisper than the average working reporter. Don't dress like Fred Astaire in "Top Hat," but don't dress like Fred Sanford in "Sanford and Son," either.

"Look the part you're hoping to play," says William German, executive editor of the *San Francisco Chronicle*. "Don't show up in a college costume, which might be jeans and a sweater. Even if you're neat enough, cotton pants make people look younger. Don't make it look like this is the first suit and necktie you've ever worn."

Women: wear a suit or dress that has subdued colors. Play it conservative. Don't walk in with a plunging neckline, high hemline, or long slits in your skirt. Avoid heavy perfume, lighten up on the jewelry, and tone down the makeup. Aim for a professional look. Several editors cite the "dressed to kill" look as a no-no for job interviews. They're looking for a reporter who is solid, down to earth, and professional.

Lay out your interview uniform a few days before the big interview and try it on. Check yourself in a full-length mirror. Do you look competent, smart, and professional? Are there any stains on the tie? Any problems? If so, take care of them now.

Take off your coat, hat, and outdoor clothing before going into an interview. Don't wear sunglasses; eye contact is important and sunglasses make you seem distant and uninterested. Don't chew gum or smoke.

WHAT SHOULD I BRING WITH ME TO AN INTERVIEW?

Put a couple of breath mints in your pocket. Bring copies of your resumé and clips, neatly inserted in an attractive folder or briefcase in case the editor doesn't have the material on hand. Bring a small notebook and pen. You may need to note special instructions from an editor.

HOW SHOULD I HANDLE QUESTIONS FROM THE EDITOR?

For each question, say something positive about yourself and, if at all possible, work in your knowledge about the paper. Don't memorize any speeches, which would make you sound forced and unnatural. But be ready to marshall your arguments during the interview.

Answer briefly, getting right to the point, without a long pause while you ponder the question. You'll appear to think well on your feet if you can do that.

Some more tips for making the most of the interview:

Sit up in your seat. Look the editor right in the eyes. Smile whenever it's appropriate. Be enthusiastic and energetic. Project self-confidence. Remember you don't just want a newspaper job. You want this newspaper job in this city because you can do something for this paper.

Does this mean putting on a false face? Not really. You are selling a product, dressing it up in its best package, but that product is you.

Don't try to be the perfect interview robot. That approach leads to disaster. That's why we've deliberately avoided giving you all-purpose "correct" answers to questions. The point of this section is to give you an idea of the questions you will face so you can reflect on them and custom design your own answers ahead of time.

Try to practice with a friend posing as the editor. Tape record the session. When you play it back, listen for the times you faltered or didn't back up your claims with compelling detail. After you're done, give it another try. You'll be astonished at how well you perform at the interview after that — no matter how nervous or shy you might feel inside.

Again and again, editors tell us the best thing an applicant can do is "be yourself." Tell your story. Don't fabricate. There's no need to.

"Many young people . . . think they have to be somebody and they don't," says Carl E. Beck Jr., editor of the *Spartanburg Herald-Journal* in South Carolina. "They just have to be themselves. It's important because if I don't like the way they really are, they won't be happy with the paper and I won't be happy with them."

WHAT ARE SOME OF THE STANDARD INTERVIEW QUESTIONS?

1. **What can you tell me about yourself?** That's your opening to talk about how and why you fell in love with journalism. Weave in an incident that demonstrates you have talent and a real passion for the profession. Don't ramble on. Two minutes is plenty. The editor is interested in what makes you tick, but he doesn't want your life story.

2. **So why do you want to be a journalist?** Editors are sick of always hearing this question answered, "Well, I always wanted to write." Say that and the editor will think you're another run-of-the-mill candidate. Your love for writing may well be one reason, but you've got to flesh the answer out. Why do you love to write? What do you hope to accomplish in the business? What kind of stories fascinate you? What makes a newspaper job seem fun to you? Why is it worth all the sacrifices?

3. **What are your strengths?** This should be easy. Just talk about

how your particular talents, experience, and education make you a strong candidate for that paper. Back up your claims with detail.

4. **What are your weaknesses?** Tougher, but put a positive spin on whatever you say. Something like, "I don't have all the daily experience in the world, but at my college paper I did (this) and (that). I have a reputation for working hard right off the bat." You can do that with other weaknesses in a resumé — education, age, whatever. Find your weakest link and then describe how you can overcompensate for it and do a terrific job.

5. **Why do you want to work for this paper?** Don't leave the impression you are looking for any old newspaper job. Here's where your research comes in. Talk about something you admire in the paper, or some praise you've heard about it. Explain why you think that paper will draw out your talents and give you an opportunity to do a bang-up job.

   Candidates should "show us they are applying to this paper and not to one of fifty newspapers," says William Handy, managing editor of *The Wichita (KS) Eagle-Beacon*.

6. **What do you think about working weekends and nights?** As a journalist, you will have crazy hours. Say you understand a journalist does not always work nine to five, and stress that you are willing to work hard whenever the editor needs you.

7. **What have you been doing with yourself since college? Or the variant: why have you been out of work for so long?** Say you've used the time well and describe how. Hopefully, you will have filled the slack time with some writing. Try to put a positive spin on what you've done and say your experience has made you a better journalist.

   Many editors are impressed with some work experience outside journalism, as long as you can make it clear it helped you as a reporter.

8. **I'm worried about your lack of daily experience.** If you have little, there's no sense trying to deny it. But you can take almost any question in a positive direction. "I know I've never worked for a daily paper, but . . ." Then talk about how you worked under deadline pressure at a weekly or with your college paper or an internship. Or about another

writing experience and your willingness to learn. Make it clear that a lack of experience with a daily newspaper is not going to hold you back from doing a terrific job for that editor.

9. **What do you like to do in your spare time?** The classic answer is: I don't expect to have much spare time, but when I get the time I like to (fill in the blank). But often, a hobby can be a good talking point and help break the ice with an editor. If you love to read, that's always a good answer. Editors recognize that good writers are often well-read. Just don't make it sound like you enjoy your hobbies more than your work. If you do, you're in the wrong profession.

10. **Why do you want to leave your current job?** Never say anything critical of your current editor or employers. Editors don't want a troublemaker in the news room. Say something positive about the company ("I really learned a lot there") but add that you feel this paper will give you a better opportunity to grow as a journalist.

11. **What sort of money are you looking for?** Say you want the job and salary is secondary. Then calmly ask what the paper pays starting reporters (or reporters with whatever level of experience you have).

    We know it's tough to put pay on the back burner. Friends will be stepping into jobs that start at $30,000 a year or more. You may make $13,000 or $14,000, sometimes even less at a small daily.

    But you shoot yourself in the foot if you hint you won't work for the going rate. First, the editor won't budge — there are usually other applicants willing to take the job at that price. Second, you'll brand yourself as someone who cares more about pay than about job satisfaction. If you do, you're getting into the wrong business. And if you say so, an editor assumes you would be a dissatisfied employee.

    We know you're interested in pay and benefits — especially if you have a big student loan to pay back after graduation. But the job comes first at this stage of the game.

    Will Fehr, editor of *The Salt Lake Tribune*, says he's not impressed "with someone who wants to know what his pension will be twenty years from now (or) when's his next raise."

    He is not alone.

"I would have a real problem with somebody who in the first five minutes starts talking about job benefits and salary and where they want to be in five years," says John Lemmon, managing editor of *The (Baltimore) Evening Sun*.

If you have experience, say you want a salary that's fair and reflects the quality of work you're doing. The salary — or, at least, the potential salary — will almost inevitably be better and bigger at a paper that's bigger and better. Unless you're in the "superstar journalist" category and will be snapped up elsewhere, there's no point leaving the impression that salary will be a sticking point.

12. **What did you think of your previous editor?** Again, don't badmouth your last editor or company, no matter how bad they were. The editor will think the same treatment will come back to haunt him. Just say you appreciated the opportunities your last editor gave you. Now, you want the chance to grow further.

13. **How long will you stay at this paper?** Editors of smaller dailies understand you'll move on after awhile. It generally isn't a good idea to throw out something like, "one year" or "two years." That suggests you're at the paper to mark time. If you're good, you'll give it all you have until you've learned all you can. Express to an editor that you will be working there as long as you are still learning and growing as a journalist.

14. **How much have your stories been edited? Or, what were your favorite and least favorite editors and why?** This is often a feeler to test whether you work well with editors. They are wary of hiring reporters who think their copy is sacrosanct and don't understand that rewriting is part of the game. Tread carefully.

Say something like, "I've never really had a problem with an editor. When I first started, I would sit down with editors (or professors) and go over my copy with them. That helped me become a sharper writer."

It's possible that many of your editors have done a poor job editing copy. But don't say that.

15. **What do you hope to be doing in five years?** This one is up to you. It depends on your personal goals.

But here's the basic idea: you want the editor to know you're not going to be a lazy blob — that you've got loads of ambition. But tell him you realize the business is not a road paved with gold. Stress that you are going to work hard to realize your dreams, and you understand you have to build your skills a day at a time.

Don't say you want to be editor of this paper in five years. Don't act like a hotshot know-it-all who isn't willing to pay your dues.

If you dream of working for a bigger paper, you can admit that. But make it clearly understood you've got a lot to learn and plan to bust your butt for this paper to become the best reporter you can be.

"People who act like they are doing us a favor by considering working for us won't get very far usually," says William Handy, managing editor of *The Wichita (KS) Eagle-Beacon.*

16. **If I give you this job, what would be your plan of attack?** To go out and break the interesting stories is your theme. Back up your claim with examples of good writing you've done previously. If you have dreamed up story ideas for that paper ahead of time, now's the time to spring them.

17. **You've come across the country for this interview. Would you have any problems relocating?** If you want the job badly: "None at all. Tell me when you want me to start and I'll be here."

HOW CAN I KEEP MY PANIC UNDER CONTROL?

No one goes into a job interview without being nervous, even scared. Editors understand that. But you can train yourself to master your fear.

"Part of the game is how well we hide our nervousness when we are seeking something we want and don't want to appear nervous," says Don Marsh, editor of *The Charleston (WV) Gazette.*

The voices inside your head can wreak havoc in an interview. "God, what a stupid thing to say." "I just don't have enough experience." "This editor hates me." Negative thoughts often bombard applicants the first time out.

But the voices are wrong. Editors aren't inside your head. You may be telling yourself you've blown the interview when editors are actually impressed with you.

Marsh recalls one time he asked a promising young journalist to take the grammar test he gives applicants.

"I wanted her to take the test after a forty-five minute conversation and she got nervous and said, 'No, I'm too tired. I've driven all day but I'll come back tomorrow.' I never heard from her again."

You don't have to lose control. Here are a few tips for appearing calm and in command during an interview:

- **Do your homework.** Prepare ahead of time and you rarely run into surprises that rattle your peace of mind. You'll be surprised how easy it is to breeze through an interview if you know what to expect.

- **Remember why you're there.** It's not the end of the world. There will always be other interviews, other newspapers, and other jobs. Even if you botch the interview — which, if you follow these tips, you won't — you will leave further along than when you started. Chalk it up to experience, a valuable commodity.

  "Relax. Have a good time. Look at it as you might go through ten interviews before you get the job YOU want," says Tom Squitieri, Washington correspondent for the *Boston Herald*.

- **Blow off some steam and then get some rest the day before the interview.** If your skin looks good and you're refreshed, you'll appear healthier and able to handle the physical challenges of the job.

  "I always believe that before a big interview, if you think you're going to have trouble resting, go out," says Squitieri. "Don't get drunk or anything like that. Exercise, play some tennis so you're tired. It will help you sleep that night."

- **Keep reciting your strengths to yourself.** On the way to the interview, remind yourself you're okay. Recognize this is no easy task, but you're willing to brave it out.

- **Arrive early for the interview.** Scout out the paper's location ahead of time and allow plenty of time that day for any problem. If you arrive fifteen minutes early, you give yourself a big advantage. You can stop in the rest room for some important preparation. Check yourself in the mirror. Comb your hair. Take a deep breath and collect your thoughts. Smile.

The bathroom also gives you a chance to get your hands into proper condition. It sounds crazy, but editors will judge you in part on the quality of your handshake. A weak, clammy, "dead fish" handshake seems feeble and inept. But a firm and gentle shake — make sure you don't crunch any bones — suggests confidence, ability, and professionalism. Some experts advise practicing with your friends to learn how to shake hands correctly. To counter "dead fish syndrome," use your rest room visit to run hot water over your hands. After drying them thoroughly — rubbing hard — your hands should be warm and dry enough for the interview.

Without that lead time, you might arrive sweaty, dusty, and breathless. That creates a terrible impression.

Never keep an editor waiting for a scheduled interview. When you're on the job, you will have to be on time or you'll miss the story. What does it tell an editor when you're late for that crucial job interview?

- **Don't let your nerves show.** Even if you are terrified, you can do a fantastic job of hiding it if you look people in the eye, smile, and don't fidget. That starts the moment you walk in the building. If you are forced to wait several minutes past your scheduled interview time, don't pace or curse in the reception area. The secretaries may be watching you. And whom are they loyal to? Right, the editor. They will sometimes report on an applicant's behavior while the editor's door was closed.

  Smile when you meet the editor. Look him straight in the eye. Shake hands firmly and say, "Hello, Mr./ Ms. (name), I'm (your name). It's a pleasure to meet you." Remember to speak up at all times and sit up. Don't pick up items on the editor's desk or appear to be nosy about papers lying there.

- **Don't view the editor as the "enemy."** Most editors don't want to see you embarrassed or nervous. They aren't out to "get you." In fact, most editors are inclined to like somebody who shares their love for journalism. Try to see them as on your side. They are looking for a good reporter and you are looking for a job.

HOW SHOULD I HANDLE CURVE BALLS?

Knock them out of the park.

Sometimes editors ask out-of-the-blue questions. When Tom Squitieri was being interviewed for the Washington correspondent slot for *The Sun* in Lowell, Massachusetts, his previous job, the paper's publisher asked whether he was a Democrat or Republican.

"I told him I don't see what that has to do with it," Squitieri says. "You're sort of talking back, but I did it politely. I said I don't expect to be paid to represent anyone's political views. I'm going to be paid to be accurate . . . Don't be afraid to disagree with someone because it might be a trick question . . . He did say, interestingly enough, 'Well, I agree with that.'"

You can learn a lot from that response.

Obviously, an editor will ask questions not on our list. Don't give an editor what you think he wants — he may ask the question to see how you react. Most editors ask legitimate questions to probe whether you are a biased or inexperienced reporter. But we won't kid you. There are some editors who enjoy lording it over starting journalists and putting them through some tough tests to see what they are made of.

SHOULD I ASK THE EDITOR ANYTHING?

Yes. Curiosity is a plus. But don't interrupt during the editor's questions. There will come a time when an editor will ask if you have any questions.

Then, ask about his philosophy of news, particularly in regard to the job you want. However, only ask a question about a subject that has not been covered.

Here are some possible questions that could give you some insight into the editor and the paper:

What are you looking for in a reporter? How many stories a week do you expect a reporter to write? How closely do your editors work with reporters? What advice can you give me? (ask this if the editor said before the interview he has no job available).

Don't ask questions you could easily have answered with a little research. For example, don't inquire about the circulation of the paper, or whether it has a Sunday edition, or who owns it. That would emphasize your lack of interest and knowledge.

But let's say you have read that the paper is rapidly

expanding. Ask the editor how the expansion will affect the paper and its employees. Or if the paper is on the brink of collapse, ask about the paper's future and what is being done to keep it alive.

"I want them to ask good questions," says Robert Giles, executive editor of *The Detroit News*. "We look for . . . someone who's going to have a lively conversation with you (and) will be interested in newspaper talk."

WILL I HAVE TO TAKE ANY TESTS?

That depends on the newspaper. Many small dailies give an applicant tests in grammar and spelling. Middle to large-sized dailies often require applicants to work a shift and cover some stories or edit copy. Some give psychological tests.

Find out what tests will be included with an interview when you make your appointment. Be sure to find out how much time the interview and tests will require so you'll know whether to make any plans for that morning or afternoon. We suggest, however, you keep the day free in case they want to take more time with you.

Be aware that editors will closely monitor you during such tests. They want to see how well you do, and how well you work with other people. They want to make sure you are not a troublemaker.

CAN I TAKE ANYONE WITH ME TO THE INTERVIEW FOR MORAL SUPPORT?

Believe it or not, some people do. But don't bring anyone with you. You've got to make it on your own.

F. Gilman Spencer, editor and senior vice president of the *New York Daily News*, recalls seeing an elderly woman sitting around the corner after interviewing one young candidate.

"Oh, that's my mother," the candidate explained.

We suggest you leave your mother out of it.

WHAT SHOULD I SAY AT THE END OF THE INTERVIEW?

There are three steps:

1. **Find out what happens next.** Avoid a "Don't call us, we'll call you" situation. Editors often get so busy they forget to let you know where you stand. When the interview ends, find out when you should call back. Get the name of the person you should call. If there's a job available, find out when the editor will make a decision. If there isn't a job available, stress that you will keep in touch.

   Again, look the editor in the eye. Thank him for his time, shake hands firmly, and say something that will remind the editor you are hot for this job, such as you're more confident than ever you could do a great job for the paper.

2. **Write a letter THAT NIGHT thanking the editor for the interview.** The sooner you write it and mail it, the better. It will keep you fresh in the editor's mind. Tell him it was a pleasure to meet him and that your meeting strengthened your belief you would do a great job there. If you are expecting a call, say you look forward to hearing from him soon. If not, say you will be in touch soon.

3. **Within a week, call the editor.** If the editor can't come to the phone, be willing to hold or ask when you could reach him. Be polite. After speaking to him, if it seems he is sincerely trying to make up his mind, give him some time. Don't call him every day. Several editors say they don't mind an applicant calling frequently to get an interview, but they resent repeated phone calls after the interview. If you were interviewed for a job opening, that editor is taking you seriously and will make a decision as soon as he can.

   However, you can try again in two or three weeks if you have not heard anything. Just don't wear it out.

   If the editor said there were no job openings at your interview, it's wise to keep in touch with him every three or four weeks by letter or phone call. You could include new clips with the letter.

Chapter 6

Victory

I HAVEN'T GOT A JOB YET. HOW CAN I BEAT THOSE POST-GRADUATION, CAN'T-FIND-A-JOB BLUES?

Depression is almost an inevitable ailment of job seekers. Nobody's skin is so tough he or she doesn't feel the prick of rejection when told, "We don't want you." And for people trying to break into journalism, it's tough out there.

"If you haven't got a job for six months after graduation, it can really destroy your morale," says Neil Morgan, editor of *The Tribune* in San Diego.

The best way to beat the blues is to keep busy with the job hunt. Retrace your campaign. Reread this book. See if any red flags pop up. Have you been doing all you can to impress an editor with your ability and energy?

If you seem solid, reconsider your targets. After beating your head against the wall trying to get a job with top newspapers, you may have to lower your sights. If you are fresh out of college and focusing on *The New York Times, The Washington Post,* and the *Los Angeles Times,* you're going to be disappointed for good reason. Pick up and read smaller, less prestigious papers and ask yourself whether you could get some good clips and learn anything there.

"In any news room situation you go into, you're going to see some bad stuff," says Marc Stern, a reporter for the Copley News Service. "(But) have your agenda when you go in there, get the experience and get out of there . . . Eventually, you're going to get a good newspaper and you're going to be learning from reporters and editors of high quality."

You may also have to start looking outside of your geographic area.

"Somewhere the decision has to be made. I'm going to get the best job available, whatever it is," says James King, retired editor of *The Seattle Times.*

Keep your options open. After considering the newspaper and its location, ask yourself whether you're too particular about the job itself. Some newspapers will offer clerk jobs if no reporting slots are available. Once you're working in the news room, you become a familiar face, which gives you a big edge when a reporter's slot opens up.

During your search, try to get some experience any way you can. Freelancing is a good option.

"You build up your string book and you're learning at the same time," says Seattle's King.

If all else fails and you take a paying job in some other field, find one that will translate to good experience for a newspaper job.

"Maybe a job in a public relations campaign (or) some community organization or political campaign where you can do a little writing," says William German, executive editor of the *San Francisco Chronicle*.

But don't give up easily.

OKAY, I DIDN'T GIVE UP. I LANDED A JOB. NOW WHAT? HOW DO I GET BETTER AND GO TO A BETTER PAPER OR BEAT?

Some things in life cannot be rushed and a successful career in journalism is one of them. Get at least a year under your belt before you start acting too big for your britches.

Sure, you may have heard of the old saying that reporting is a young person's profession. But most people who say that are "old" reporters who want to be editors, columnists; jobs that pay more. A good reporter must have energy, dedication, and a curious mind. You don't suddenly lose those qualities at the age of thirty, forty, or fifty.

Indeed, many outstanding reporters are in their forties and fifties. Bob Woodward, who is in his forties, is still breaking stories about presidential mischief for *The Washington Post*. And Sam Donaldson, the over-fifty leather-lunged White House reporter for ABC-TV, hasn't lost any of his aggressiveness.

Woodward and Donaldson use the experience they've acquired to stay a step ahead of rival gumshoes. And they are still hungry. You can see it in their work. Donaldson gets a kick out of watching the president put his foot in his mouth. For he knows he has done his job — and as well as or better than anyone else.

But, of course, even a Sam Donaldson can burn out after spending year after year holding the president's feet to the fire. Age has little to do with it. You get tired of doing the same thing over and over.

If you decide to leave reporting, many options will be available — city editor, features editor, columnist, editorial writer, managing editor, editor-in-chief, publisher, and so on. And those jobs are held by people in all age brackets.

This is not a young person's profession. It's a business in which you can plan to work until you retire if you so desire.

Think of your first year as laying the foundation of a home. If the foundation is not solid, the entire building will fall and you will have to look for another place to live. But if you get the foundation right, you will have a home for as long as you want.

Improve your writing, interviewing technique, and reporting. Try to learn about layout and design. Once you have mastered the basics, you can build on them and perhaps specialize in a certain subject or skill. But don't get ahead of yourself. It will happen soon enough.

"You shouldn't go to Wichita and think about how much you want to go to Kansas City," says Jay Harris, executive editor of the *Philadelphia Daily News.* "That will affect how you do in Wichita. If I'm an editor in Kansas City, what's going to make me want to hire you? Not how much you want to be here, but how well you did in Wichita."

Now, with the lecture aside, there are some things you can do to further your improvement in your first year. But don't do them at the expense of learning the basics because you will have to pay the bill later.

Here are five tips:

1. **Establish a close relationship with your editors.** Ask them for advice. Don't overdo it, but show you are interested in improving. Many a successful career took off after an editor decided to take a young reporter under his wing.

2. **Try to cover a wide range of stories.** Many newspaper executives realize young reporters need a variety of experiences and put them on the general assignment beat at first. They will do all kinds of writing — features, breaking news, and perhaps obits. But if your paper assigns you to

a beat, ask for some general assignment work when you have the opportunity.

And then, see what kind of story you handle best. It could be science, politics, or perhaps police work. In a few years, you might consider making that your specialty.

3. **A few months after you begin work, ask your editors how you can improve.** They might suggest working on your feature writing or meeting deadlines. Whatever, request to do as much as you can to improve that weakness. You will improve and your editors will take note.

4. **If you are given a beat, ask the person who had the assignment before for his advice.** If you are lucky, the reporter will introduce you to his best sources and give you some story ideas.

5. **Make a contact with an editor for whom you want to work after you leave your first job.** Send a letter to him and explain you want to work there in the future. Tell him you will send clips occasionally. When you decide to leave your first job, you may have something already lined up.

HOW LONG SHOULD I STAY AT MY FIRST JOB?

Wendy Benjaminson was bright, talented, and ambitious. She grew up among newspaper people — her older brother Peter was a reporter for the *Detroit Free Press* and the coauthor of *Investigative Reporting*, a guide for reporters. She had a reporter's way of thinking, always curious, looking for the real story. Not surprisingly, she showed star ability on her college newspaper at the University of Maryland.

Shortly after college, she got a job as a reporter for *The Washington Times* and quickly moved up the ladder. Within a year, she had covered the Virginia state capital in Richmond and the city hall beat in the District of Columbia. She frequently scooped her older and more experienced rivals at *The Washington Post*.

At the age of twenty-three, she had it all, or so it seemed.

She was not happy. She felt she wasn't learning as fast as she should. One of her editors was, well, like a Mississippi summer — always hot, sometimes stormy, and frequently cursed. An emotional person, he was not very consistent in his editing and story consultation. Consequently, she was getting mixed signals and began to wonder just what she was accomplishing. Sure, she was going up the ladder, but to where?

After a little more than a year, she decided that *The Washington Times* was no longer the best place for her. She began scouting around and finally landed a job as a metro reporter for the United Press International office in Washington, DC. She again impressed her editors and moved ahead. Within a year, she was named an editor on the national desk of UPI.

Benjaminson made the right move. But how did she know? Why did she leave? She had the respect of her peers and superiors at the time and no doubt would have continued to advance at *The Times*. For someone twenty-three years old, it was a gamble.

"I just felt I had gotten to the point where I couldn't learn anymore," she explains.

That says it all. Whether it's your first job or your twenty-first, when you stop learning, start looking.

"You think: can I learn here?" says Don Marsh, editor of *The Charleston (WV) Gazette*. "Do I like what I'm doing? Are the people nice? If the answers are no, I think you start looking soon."

You have to be careful, though. Editors say you should try to stay at your first job for at least one year. Make the jump to the big time, but don't get a reputation as a job hopper. If you are bouncing from one job to the next, an editor might wonder if you have a problem.

Before you decide to leave, be sure you have hit a dead end. Don't leave because you got mad at your editor one day.

"If you can stick it out, it's better," says Benjaminson, who made it past the one-year point. "They (editors) don't like you to job hop. But you do get to a point where you can't learn anymore."

"I'm real leery of people who skip around a bit," agrees N. Christian Anderson, editor of *The Orange County (CA) Register*.

Hopefully, you won't worry about how long you should stay at your first job. If you are hired by the right paper, you could be set for life.

"I started as a copy boy at the newspaper I work for," says Will Fehr, who is now editor of *The Salt Lake Tribune*.

If you are not so lucky, we recommend asking yourself the following questions before you leave:

1. **Am I being challenged?** If not, can you ask your editors for help? They might shift you to another beat or give you different assignments.

2. **Does your current position offer you an opportunity for advancement?** Will you get a better beat if you improve? Or is your beat just leaving you "beat" at the end of the day?

3. **Are your editors — and/or the quality of the paper — holding you back?** How much has your editor helped you since you came to work? Do you think you would learn more if you moved to another paper?

4. **Can you get a better job?** You may not be learning much, but what are your options? Do you have the clips and experience to do better? If the answer is yes, go for it. If not, look harder for ways to stay sharp.

   Whatever you decide, do not leave your current job before getting another one. It's easier to get a job if you already have one.

HOW DO I GO UP THE LADDER? WHAT IF I WANT TO BE AN EDITOR, A WASHINGTON REPORTER, A COLUMNIST, ETC.?

A Case History

N. Christian Anderson was named editor of *The Orange County (CA) Register*, which has a circulation on Sunday of more than 325,000, eight years after he graduated from college.

He was not lucky. He was not even the son of the publisher. How did he do it?

Anderson started working for a newspaper when most boys his age were happy to deliver one. He was in the seventh grade when he got a job writing shorts for a weekly paper called *The Heppner Gazette Times* in his hometown in Oregon. It didn't take him long to get hooked.

"I never had any doubt that I wanted to be in this business," says Anderson.

So Anderson, while hooked, was not a fish out of water. He loved newspapers from the beginning and he knew that's what he wanted to do with his life.

That's lesson one of this case history: if you know where you want to go, it's easier to get there.

As a freshman in high school, Anderson became sports editor for *The Heppner Gazette Times*. And as if he didn't have enough to do, he worked for his high school newspaper. He was acquiring experience most people do not get until college, if then.

After high school, Anderson landed a summer internship with a newspaper in Albany, Oregon.

Lesson number two: contacts.

He later worked part-time for the Albany paper while attending Oregon State University and was named the assistant city editor after graduation. Six months later, he was named city editor.

He kept that post for almost three years when he became editor of a paper in Walla Walla, Washington, which is owned by *The Seattle Times*.

Lesson number three: he took a job with a company that had growth potential.

After two years at Walla Walla, he was invited to work for *The Seattle Times* as an assistant to the executive editor. He later was named associate managing editor in charge of graphics and feature operations.

And, he made such a good impression he was offered the job of editor of the *Register* just two years later.

You don't have to work in the seventh grade to get anywhere in this business. Anderson is obviously a special person. But he also made all the right moves. And, most importantly, he realized he needed to start on the bottom to get to the top.

The moral of the story: to be an "overnight" success, work long nights over and over again. There's no alternative to hard work.

And if you are interested in a certain position, let your editor know and do some research on that subject. For example, if you want to go to Washington, read about national affairs. Try to do some stories that have a Washington or national slant. If your paper has a Washington bureau, establish a relationship with the bureau chief and the reporters. Volunteer to help them research something back home if needed. This can pay off later when they are considering promoting someone to Washington.

The same technique applies if you want to be an editor or whatever. Let your superiors know you are interested. Ask them what you need to do to accomplish your goal. Then, follow that path.

IS WORKING FOR A NEWSPAPER WORTH THE TROUBLE?

Many people in this business would say if you have to ask that question, you belong somewhere else. You either love it or your don't.

"It's the best business in the f------ world," says F. Gilman Spencer of the *New York Daily News*. "It saved my life. It's saved a lot of people's lives."

Spencer, whose language is more salty than the midpoint of the Atlantic Ocean, is a newspaper success story if there ever was one. He has done a little of everything — sports editor, news reporter, city editor, photographer, and now he's editor of a daily newspaper read by millions. But he was on the bottom when he drifted into the business.

"I got thrown out of the house by my mother . . . and wasn't going to school and ended up as a copy editor with a newspaper, the *Inquirer* in Philadelphia," says Spencer.

Spencer feels he owes his life to journalism.

That's a strange statement, isn't it? Owe your life to a profession, a job? How many people in other fields might say that? But it's a common sentiment in journalism.

Sure, it pays talented people less than what they could get in other professions. The hours stink and more than one marriage has fallen apart because a reporter spent more time with his source than his spouse.

"It's probably hurt my personal life a little bit," says Tom Squitieri, Washington correspondent for the *Boston Herald*. "Any journalist will tell you that."

But we make the sacrifices.

Why?

We have a responsibility to inform people of the day's events — honestly, accurately, and fairly. And it is not a responsibility taken lightly. That's why you see us standing in the rain, notebook in hand, waiting for the mayor to show up so we can get a comment. That's why we work nights and weekends when our friends in other businesses are home watching television or at the beach. And that's why we stay on the job after we are offered a major salary boost at the public relations firm up the street.

But it's not all sacrifice.

There's nothing like breaking a story on deadline. Your editors are jumping up and down. The adrenaline is pumping. It's a great feeling!

Still, it is a reasonable question to ask: is it worth it?

It must seem that we have advised you to do everything but jump through a hoop. Your resumé should be just so and your clips should be such a way. And don't mess up in the interview. And so on.

It does give one pause. After all, if you can be successful in journalism, you can do well in many other professions. So before you take the plunge, it is wise to think about what you want to do with your life. Is money the most important thing? Do you want a nine-to-five job?

But consider this: the newspaper business is filled with lively, interesting, dedicated, and exciting people. There's something about this business that brings out the best in you.

One of your coauthors recalls the time when he was trying to get a job with States News Service, a wire service based in Washington, DC. He went in for an interview, but was told there wouldn't be an opening for a month.

He called back a month later, but didn't get the job. However, he was told there might be another opening in a few weeks.

He didn't get that one, either.

It looked bleak, especially since he was unemployed at the time. After about four months, the managing editor told him to call on a certain day about yet another opening.

He called, but the managing editor had a bad case of the flu and was at home in bed. Try back in a week or two, he was told.

Your coauthor figured he had nothing to lose. He had been trying to get a job with this place for four months. So he called the managing editor at home.

"Hi, Peter. How are you doing?"

"I'm sick."

"Yeah, I heard. Uh . . . you said to give you a call today? I was just wondering how does it look?"

"Phil, you must want this job pretty badly . . ."

"Well, yeah . . ."

"All right, come on in next week."

He showed up for work. Early in the morning the first

day, the editor-in-chief came running up to him with a wild look in his eye.

"Did you call Peter out of his sickbed?"

"Uh, I guess I did."

"Good for you," the editor said.

On behalf of all editors around the country, we do not recommend you call one out of his sickbed. But the story shows how much your coauthor wanted to get that job, which paid just $170 a week to start. He knew in his heart what he wanted to do.

Nothing else mattered.

Case Histories: The Way It Is

Now that we've walked you through the techniques of landing a job, it's time to look at how journalists have actually used those techniques to land jobs.

As you will see, everybody's story is different. There is no one path to a journalism job. Some star journalists hold master's degrees; others don't have a college education. Some used contacts to land a position; other answered advertisements.

We've included stories by newspaper journalists who have moved on to other fields: a governor's press secretary, a producer of a television news show, a journalism professor. We've included stories by journalists running the gamut from a reporter on her first job at a suburban weekly to a veteran editor.

We hope their stories will illustrate how the techniques we've outlined can work in real life. And we hope they'll do something more: show you that, while it's tough out there, you can make it, too.

JOB: Editor, Lawrence (MA) Eagle-Tribune

NAME: Daniel J. Warner

AGE IN 1988: 51

HOMETOWN: Worthington, Ohio

EDUCATION: One year, Ohio State University

FIRST JOB: Sportswriter, The Sharon (OH) Spectator

HOW DID YOU GET WHERE YOU ARE TODAY?

"My first job was as sportswriter on a hometown weekly, *The Sharon Spectator*. It lasted . . . not long. I did that for a couple years, right out of high school. I also worked in the circulation department, that sort of thing. It was owned by a crazy woman lawyer who had it for fun, and we had a lot of fun (laughing).

"Then I went to Ohio State for a year. I was having a lot of family problems. The grandmother I grew up with was dying. I just wanted to do something, so I went to work for *The (Elyria, OH) Chronicle-Telegram* as a suburban reporter covering a whole bunch of little communities — my memory is, like, nine to twelve little farm towns. I would drive all over the place, and do everything from type up handwritten correspondence to do features, and all that kind of thing. They were having trouble finding people, so the job was, frankly, fairly easy to come by.

"I worked there for four or five years, went in the Army, got out of the Army, and got a job for the (Akron, OH) *Beacon Journal*. I started as a suburban bureau reporter, did that for a year, became a roving suburban reporter for a year or so, worked as an assignment editor on the suburban desk, went to the city desk and worked a whole bunch of beats — medicine, labor, city hall. Then I went to the Sunday department, wrote for the Sunday magazine for a couple of years, became suburban editor and then city editor. And then, right before I left in '69, I became managing editor.

"I came to Lawrence (MA) as managing editor. (Laughing, Warner says he had no secret technique for landing the job.) "I answered an ad in *Editor and Publisher* — about the most traditional and scorned way you can think of, right? They had over 100 applications. It helps to learn how to talk. I mean, you've got to sell yourself in an interview. Contacts don't hurt, but that isn't how I got here."

(After six months on the job, Warner had an offer to work on the *Philadelphia Inquirer*.) "I got to Philadelphia because they knew me . . . (the chain) which owned Akron, bought the *Inquirer*, and they were looking to put together a team in Philadelphia. They talked to me about that. And I said, 'Sure, that sounds like a hell of a challenge.' I organized their suburban bureau system, which they had none of at the time. Then I was news editor, then night managing editor. After three years, I came to Lawrence as managing editor, and then became editor eight years later.

"Somewhere along the line I developed the ethic, I guess, the concept, that everybody in a news room is a reporter — essentially, like everybody in the Army is a rifleman. Everybody in a news room is basically a reporter and thinks and acts and walks and talks and has the goals of a reporter. My various reporting experiences are really the basis for what I do. And that's why we're here. Everything else is sort of bull. Being city editor was sort of the epitome of being a reporter for me. It was a big, long high for me. It was like having all these arms and legs out there reporting. They'd come and talk to me, and I'd talk to them, and we'd wrestle over it. It was exciting times in Akron. I was city editor through a race riot. We had great political upheaval. The town was trying to revitalize itself in a way that had a lot of governmental action going. There was a lot of action, and when there wasn't action, we were creating it. It imbued me with the belief that news rooms are constantly active.

"In Philadelphia, some people there . . . gave some sense of quality and values that I had never had. There were some people there who were, frankly, better than anything I had run into before. I handled the major stories for Sunday, which meant editing a couple guys . . . who have won several Pulitzers for in-depth investigations. What a challenge, to edit those guys! They taught me that you really could get into things in ways that I never dreamed possible. It just taught me, by using your instincts and your imagination, you can make things happen.

"I think (to make it in this business) you have to be willing to take risks . . . Going to Philadelphia (for example). I had just moved my family, I had just gotten a good job with a company that was great to me. But going there gave me a measure of sophistication and ability that I think added an edge."

(Warner returned to the managing editor's post in Lawrence after three years in Philadelphia.) "Frankly, there was an area where I matched my personal life against my professional life. I was headed for divorce in Philadelphia. I was going to work at eleven in the morning and coming home at one or two in the morning. I really made a conscious decision to balance those, and I think those are the kinds of decisions you have to make in a career."

TIPS FOR YOUNG JOURNALISTS ASPIRING TO BE EDITORS

"Be a reporter.

"This is going to sound trite, but you've got to care about reporting. To be a great editor, a good editor, you have to believe that what you do has value — as opposed to people who apologize for what they do. It isn't in my vocabulary that we invade people's privacy. I don't believe we do that. I hear people saying it at meetings, and if I believed that, I'd get out of the business. You've got to believe in what you do to the point that the doubts don't get in your way. If you have basic doubts, forget it. I advise people to really think about what they want to do, and really run it through their ethic system and their mind. I really think it's important to understand what we do and believe in it.

"I think that in this business — maybe unlike any other — the best managers are those who are thoroughly grounded in the craft themselves. This business is full of so many good people, and also so many egos, that you've got to be good at what you do, or you're not going to be followed. I think there are models in other businesses where you don't have to be good at the business — that you can be good at managing."

(Warner also says experience at a metropolitan daily is invaluable.) "You know, this is going to be controversial. I think the world is full of small-town journalism, and journalists who practice small-town journalism. And they never get better. They do the same thing, over and over and over again. I worry about that with me. You know, I've been here fifteen years. But I think having done that was a big leg up because it broadened my horizon. Mainly from . . . the editor chewing my ass. He used to say things like, 'God damn it, you're smarter than that,' or 'We can be smarter than *The New York Times*, let's go do this.' And we'd go do it. He had the ability and the practice of journalism to go along with it. Some of the reporting techniques and the writing techniques — they come back to me almost out of the subconscious. When I run into a situation, I think of solutions that I don't think I would have thought of without that.

"The papers I subscribe to, to model, aren't papers our size. They're metros."

JOB: City Editor, the *Corpus Christi Caller-Times*

NAME: Nick Jiminez

AGE IN 1988: 45

HOMETOWN: San Antonio, Texas

EDUCATION: Graduated from Baylor University in 1966. Worked briefly for his campus newspaper and had a summer internship with the *Edinburg Daily Review*, a small daily in south Texas.

FIRST JOB: Reporter for the *Edinburg Daily Review*

HOW DID YOU GET WHERE YOU ARE TODAY?

"In my senior year, the guy who was teaching my journalism course had a friend of his who had just bought the paper in Edinburg. My teacher said the publisher needed someone down there who could speak Spanish. I was going to be a lifeguard somewhere so I decided to go down there instead. (The paper hired Jiminez after his internship.) It shows what you can do if you have a contact. The other thing is that I may have been the only Mexican-American who was taking journalism courses at the time at Baylor. And this guy just happened to buy a paper down by the Rio Grande Valley (which has a large Spanish-speaking population). It was good timing."

Jiminez, however, worked for the Edinburg paper for just three months because he was drafted by the Army.

"I was in the Army for about two years. The reason I got (his second job, as a reporter for the *Corpus Christi Caller-Times*,) was that when I was down there in the Valley, I got to know a reporter for the *Caller-Times*. They had a bureau in the Valley then. Once, the editor (of the *Caller-Times*) came down and the reporter introduced me. So, when I went into the army, the reporter suggested I write the editor a letter when I got out. So I did. About two days later, he called me up and offered me a job."

Jiminez had worked as a reporter for the *Caller-Times* for about ten years ("covering everything from A to Z") when a news editor one day asked him what he wanted to do to further his career.

"I said, I want to know what you do. And he suggested I sit with him for a few days. I wasn't thinking about becoming a city editor at the time. I just wanted to learn, to become acquainted with the desk. So I sat up on the desk for a couple of days and it just kind of evolved. He asked me to help out and take over sometimes. I just kind of hung on that way when (a new city editor for the afternoon edition of the paper) was hired. The editor decided he needed an assistant city editor. So I applied. I figured I knew the job. I knew all the beats in the news room and I had acquired experience on the desk . . . I got the job."

Two years later, the city editor was promoted to managing editor.

"That really helped out. I was under a guy who was going places. That's always good because if he moves up, you can move up. I became city editor right after that."

TIPS FOR BECOMING A CITY EDITOR

"You need to be acquainted with all parts of the paper. I came into the business to write and report, which is fine. But you look at things from a different perspective from the city desk. You look at the whole organism, from reporting to production . . . If you are a reporter, work on projects where more than one person is involved — team projects. Try to be a team leader. This gives you some management experience . . . But more than anything, tell people what you want to do. A lot of people think that management knows everything. But unless you've told people what you want to do, they may not think about you when the job opens up. Let people know what your ambitions are. They can't divine it."

JOB: Staff photographer, *Newsday*

NAME: Julia Gaines

AGE IN 1988: 37

HOMETOWN: Kensington, MD

EDUCATION: Graduated from the University of Maryland in 1978. Journalism degree. Worked as a staff photographer for the campus newspaper.

FIRST JOB: Part-time staff photographer for the *Prince George's (MD) Journal,* which was then a twice-weekly newspaper.

HOW DID YOU GET WHERE YOU ARE TODAY?

"When I was still in college, I applied for a job with the *Prince George's Journal* and (a friend who was more experienced) did too. But I got the job. I was taking fewer classes than he was, and the *Journal* was looking for a college student who had the time to work twenty to thirty hours a week."

Gaines says she was told later by her boss that he was impressed with her pictures, which showed creativity and variety. She worked for the *Journal* during her final year in school.

"I was the number two person to the chief photographer. I got a lot of experience doing high school sports, features, and learning to process color slides."

While looking for full-time work after college, Gaines interviewed with *The Washington Star,* which needed a good freelancer to shoot high school sports.

"I did that and it escalated into other assignments. Then I was told there was an opening for a part-time lab technician (at the *Star*). I took it and it turned into a full-time job ... One of the main reasons (they hired her) was that they saw how dependable I was. They said I was someone they could trust . . . I still got photography assignments, but it took about two years before I was put on the staff as a photographer. Then about eight months later the paper folded."

After *The Star's* demise, Gaines began freelancing for *The Washington Post, The (Cleveland) Plain Dealer* and the Associated Press. This paid the bills and provided job leads.

"It kept me in touch with other photographers to find out what jobs were open."

Early in 1982, *The Washington Times,* which was due to begin publication, hired Gaines without looking at her portfolio on the recommendations of several ex-*Star* photographers and writers who had signed on at the paper. Gaines had worked at *The Times* for about two years when the former photography director at *The Star* suggested she apply to *Newsday.* He was now an assistant managing editor at *Newsday.*

Newsday requires an applicant to work on a five-day tryout, which Gaines did on her vacation. The paper wasn't hiring then, but she knew it would be within a year because of increased staffing on its New York city edition.

"They called me about a year later. I had the job."

TIPS FOR LANDING A JOB AS A PHOTOJOURNALIST

"While in college, don't just take photography classes in the journalism department. I took photography classes in the art, design, architecture, and even the physics department. A good background in government and politics is important because a photographer covers everything from the local mayor's office to the White House. Everything you learn can be useful, especially current events. It's good to be versatile. You have to be at home shooting both in the studio and on the sidelines shooting sporting events."

JOB: Political reporter, the *Delaware State News*

NAME: Virginia Kirk

AGE IN 1988: 26

HOMETOWN: Laurel, MD

EDUCATION: Graduated from George Washington University in 1984 with journalism degree. Was editor of the campus newspaper. Had internship with the Washington bureau of Harte-Hanks Newspapers.

FIRST JOB: Reporter for the *Bryan-College Station (TX) Eagle*

HOW DID YOU GET YOUR START IN JOURNALISM?

"I sent out my resumés to some papers, including one in the company for which I was an intern. I met the editor when he was in Washington. He told me to send a resumé and he offered me a job. There were people in the company who were pulling for me, putting in a good word."

Kirk had worked as a reporter for the *Eagle* for two and a half years when she decided to leave.

"The economy in Bryan was hurting. It looked like there wouldn't be any raises for awhile. I felt like I needed to go to a bigger paper and do some bigger stories. So I just left without another job and went to Europe for a month.

"I was really interested in working for a bigger paper, but I applied for a job with the *Delaware State News*, which had an ad in *Editor and Publisher*. (The circulation of the *Delaware State News*, which is based in Wilmington, is about the same as the *Eagle*.) They offered me a job as a political reporter, covering state politics and the capital. So I decided to take it. I've covered two presidential candidates, the state capital, and the senate races. It's a small paper, but I am getting great experience. That will help me later.

"When I left the *Eagle*, I also wanted to work for a paper that had some competition. The *Eagle* is the only paper in Bryan. But we are up against the (*Wilmington Evening Journal*). You have them looking over your shoulder. You can compare your stories against theirs. That makes you work harder and faster."

TIPS FOR LANDING YOUR SECOND JOB

"I think you should look to get as much experience as possible after college. Don't worry about working for a big paper. Look for a place where you can learn, where you will have freedom to do some good stories. Even though I didn't go to a bigger paper, I got to meet a lot more people covering state and national politics. I wouldn't have done that if I had gone to a bigger paper.

"Also, work for a paper that is competitive. That's the best way to improve."

JOB: Medical reporter, *USA Today*

NAME: Tim Friend

AGE IN 1988: 32

EDUCATION: Graduated in 1984, University of Missouri, bachelor's degree in journalism

HOMETOWN: Springfield, MO

FIRST JOB: Assistant editor of a weekly, *The Centralia (MO) Fireside Guard*

HOW DID YOU GET WHERE YOU ARE TODAY?

"I went to college out of high school for two years, majored in biology and chemistry — actually, mostly in beer and women. I was working part-time for a law firm while I was in school, then I went full-time for them, just as a messenger and librarian for about six months. Then I became a traveling insurance salesman. I made a lot of money, and just continued to enjoy myself, carrying on the party we started in college. I did that for about a year and a half.

"Then I moved back to my hometown, and started working as an O.R. tech (operating room technician) in a hospital, assisting in surgery, passing instruments, that sort of thing. I had gotten that job, actually, as a senior in high school. I had gotten on-the-job training and worked about forty hours a week on the evening shift, so I essentially went back to the job I had before.

"I stayed in the O.R. for almost six years. I spent the last four years of that on an open heart team.

"By about age twenty-six, I finally figured out what I wanted to do. I always enjoyed writing, and I liked writing fiction. Initially, I decided if I was going to become a good fiction writer, the best thing I could do would be to get a job writing full-time. And newspaper work seemed to be the best opportunity for that. So I applied to journalism school and got in, started when I was about twenty-seven, and was there for two years.

"I graduated and did purgatory at the weekly newspaper . . . I took the job in February of 1985, left in late June. The problem that I had graduating at age twenty-nine was that I did not feel I had time, nor did I have the inclination, to start out at a mid-sized daily and work my way up for the next five years to be eventually allowed to write medical stories. I knew that already I knew more about medicine than most reporters that I would meet, and it really kind of irritated me that I couldn't get a newspaper to hire me as a medical writer. I figured out pretty quickly that I was going to get the same answer everywhere I went: 'You're going to have to start out as a police beat reporter.' Well, when I was in journalism school, I didn't have the luxury of being able to take off the summer and go to a $3-an-hour internship, which is the way people get a lot of jobs. I could make, just working part-time (in the operating room), $12,000 to $14,000 a year.

"When I got out, one of my professors suggested I might try this job at the *Fireside Guard* and that would get me over the hump. It would be intensive training, because it was essentially a one-man show. I was the chief reporter, chief photographer, chief copy editor, chief layout person. It was pretty good experience, and I wouldn't trade that at all. It was really rather valuable. I think I learned in four months at that weekly what a lot of people gain at a less intensive job at a mid-sized daily in a year. I was working my butt off, covering police beat, school beat, city council, the whole thing — just good, basic reporting. But I felt really lost in that job, wasting my skills.

"We moved out here (Washington, DC) blind, without jobs. My wife was from Washington, so we at least had a place to stay. We arrived on a Saturday, and in the Sunday *Post,* in the want ads, there was a job for a medical journalist.

"I sent out two resumés when I got to Washington: one to a hospital association, a p.r. job offering $26,000 a year to start. They offered me the job. I also applied at the medical reporting job, which was the International Medical News Group, and they offered me $16,000 to start. So I chose the one that offered $16,000 — simply because my instincts told me that if I veered off the path at that point, it would be very difficult to ever come back.

"The International Medical News Group publishes six physician newspapers, or trade journals, for different specialties. My job was traveling to medical conferences around the country and writing up the scientific medical papers that they present as news stories, in as plain English as possible for doctors. It was very intensive. In a sense, it gave me kind of a free post-graduate medical education. I would attend these sessions from start to finish. There may be fifteen to twenty presentations made at a three-day meeting, and I would come back and write maybe ten to fifteen stories from the meeting.

"I was in that cycle of attending meetings, coming back, writing my ten or fifteen stories, going to another meeting and coming back. I did that for about eighteen months. Then I got frustrated again with the income I was making. My wife had gotten pregnant in the meantime, and we'd had a child.

"One of my classmates was working at a health association here in town and she convinced me that I should come over and try her job. She was getting married and moving to Philadelphia. They were offering $28,000, and by that time I was making $22,000. So a $6,000 increase and a chance to buy a house – that kind of thing weighed heavily.

"I took the job and realized I had made a mistake the first day I was there. Again, my instincts. I knew that I had strayed from my goal of becoming a medical writer for a daily newspaper.

"I continued to freelance for the International Medical News Group, worked at this job at the trade association for about three months, and then my former employer offered me $28,000 to come back.

"During this time, the medical writer at *USA Today* was leaving to go to *U.S. News and World Report*. He used to work at the International Medical News Group about four years ago, and he had called my managing editor. I hadn't actually left the trade association yet, so they didn't have anything to lose by referring the medical writer to me.

"I sent in a resumé, interviewed for the job, and made it through all the cuts. During my interview, they asked me if I could write brief, concise stories. I told them, 'I think medicine should be administered in small doses.' I think that impressed them.

"It was down to me and one other person. This guy was already with the Gannett newspaper system. Even though I had probably more practical medical experience and background than he did, he was in the Gannett system and he got the job. But the editors liked me, so they suggested that I maybe freelance for them or just keep in touch from time to time.

"After I didn't get the job, I went back to INMG. About a month and a half after going back, *USA Today* called me and said that the writer didn't work out. He had gone back to his old job, mostly for personal reasons. Would I be interested in coming back for a tryout?

"I went in over the Thanksgiving holidays, and worked Thanksgiving Day, Friday, Sunday, and took Monday off from my job — a four-day tryout. Actually, it was really terrifying. I did my one story on Thursday. On Friday, the pace picked up a little bit. I had a couple of stories that had to be done on deadline — things that broke at 5 o'clock in the afternoon, and I had half an hour to get the story finished. I was able to show them I could do it. Those things that happened were actually bad things - but good for me because I proved myself.

"After I finished my trial on Monday, I went back to my job on Tuesday. They said they'd call me in a few days. So the next three days were miserable — sleepless nights.

"On Wednesday, I had lunch with a friend. I was telling him everything that I had been banking on was on the line. I had always believed that if I could find the right editor, and had a chance to prove myself, I could show someone it would be worthwhile to hire me. If I didn't get the job, I was wrong all along. I didn't know what I would do if I didn't get the job. It would mean I was wrong, there was no way I could ever become a medical writer unless I went to some newspaper and paid my dues as a twenty-two year old would have.

"Thursday, *USA Today* called me and offered me the job.

"For me, it's perfect. I'm a little bit evangelical in wanting to give information to people to make them more aware so they can challenge their doctors about whether they're getting the right treatment or not. With *USA Today*, it's got five and a half million readers every day, and it makes a difference."

TIPS FOR JOURNALISTS WHO WANT TO DO SPECIALIZED REPORTING

"I would recommend getting into something where you can really polish your journalism skills and learn more about your particular specialty.

"If you're young enough, go the standard route with a small daily newspaper. I'm not saying I'm great or anything, but without (that experience) you really have to be an exception. You have to work twice as hard as everybody else in your office so that you really are qualified for that job when the opportunity comes up. I don't understand all of the inherent biases against trade reporters, but there is an arrogance among newspaper editors that unless you started at a newspaper there's no way you can understand what the job is all about.

"The two editors that I tried out under really did go to bat for me when it came down to deciding whether they were going to hire me or not. Essentially, the managing editors had their doubts. They were really pretty dubious about bringing in somebody as green as I was — green in terms of newspaper work. But the editors said, 'Trust us. This is the guy we need.'

"Then it was up to me not to screw up."

JOB: Wire service reporter, New York state capital bureau

NAME: Jonathan Ferziger

AGE IN 1988: 27

HOMETOWN: The Bronx, New York City, NY

EDUCATION: Graduated from Columbia University in 1984. Majored in journalism. Worked on the campus newspaper while attending the State University of New York. Started own campus newspaper at State University. Had an internship with *Community Jobs,* a Washington, DC-based monthly employment guide.

FIRST JOB: News clerk in Paris bureau of United Press International

HOW DID YOU GET WHERE YOU ARE TODAY?

"After journalism school I was pretty sure I didn't want to be a journalist. So I went to France. I worked as a waiter for awhile and I was selling newspapers on the street. Then I got a (three month) internship with the *International Herald Tribune.* Then I had some odd jobs. Just when I was about to run out of money, I heard from some friends that United Press International needed some very cheap labor. So I started bothering them for a month. I finally got a job as a news clerk, filing stories and making phone calls. They needed people so I started writing sports copy. I stayed there Friday nights to cover French soccer . . . Then it happened that Rock Hudson came to France for AIDS treatment one Friday night when I was covering soccer. I went up to the hospital and I stayed on that story for the next week. I got great clips from that . . . It's funny. You get in the right position and the breaks just happen.

"I came back to the states and I showed my clips (on Rock Hudson) and I got hired in UPI's New York city bureau. I was there for about five or six months. I was mostly an editor, but I covered police stories. I came up here (UPI's bureau in Albany, NY) to do mostly editing and a little reporting. The way the wire service is set up, the more you stick with it, the more reporting you can do. You start off doing feature stories, book reviews, weekend travel pieces. Then when you see an interesting issue, you go for it.

"Once I was in Albany, I figured it would be pretty frustrating to come out of here without covering the capital. I directed myself to try to figure out what was going on here. I looked for assignments that got me close to the capital. Eventually enough people quit that I was able to move up . . . It's funny. When I first went to work for UPI, it was just after (the wire service declared bankruptcy). But I figured that even if it went down the tubes in six months, I would have six months of experience. And, gosh, it's been three years now."

TIPS FOR LANDING A WIRE SERVICE JOB

"Bug people and keep on bugging them. Don't be a pest, but make a lot of phone calls. If you see something you like, call or write a letter. Then call five or ten more times. It's not like asking for a date. They keep your name on file. If you keep it up, they will remember you. If you are good, they will encourage you. If you are no good, they will tell you to go away."

JOB: Investigative reporter with Jack Anderson's syndicated column

NAME: Stewart Harris

AGE IN 1988: 28

EDUCATION: Graduated in 1982 from Boston University, B.S., major in journalism

HOMETOWN: St. Paul, MN

FIRST JOB: Police beat reporter in Waltham, MA for *The Middlesex News*

HOW DID YOU GET A JOB AS AN INVESTIGATIVE REPORTER?

"I had an internship with Jack Anderson in the summer of 1985. I got a leave of absence from *The Middlesex News*, where I had worked my way up to covering their biggest town and their most important town, Framingham.

"I was getting very bored there, and was looking around for other work when I stumbled across this ad in *Editor and Publisher* for interns for Jack Anderson, paid internships. I was sitting there in the *Middlesex News* news room, and I opened up this *E & P* and was looking through the positions offered, and I stumbled on this thing and said, 'Wow! Jack Anderson! Holy shit!' So I showed it to (two other reporters) and they both looked at it and said, 'Oh, $250 a week. Forget it. That stinks. Are you kidding me?' And I said, 'But you missed the whole point, man. This is Jack Anderson!' Nobody could get excited about it. So I said, 'Well, maybe something's wrong with my head.'

"Anyway, I sent some clips in there and got a call back. They said, 'Yeah, we actually only have one position that's paid, and we're pretty much set on giving it to this guy who's got a master's from the University of Missouri, and he's worked for *The (Newark) Star-Ledger*. We're going to give that to him, but we have unpaid positions, too. Would you be interested in one of those?' I said, 'Oh, jeez, I couldn't possibly. I've got a dog to support, and a girlfriend. I've got to take her out once a week.' And the guy . . . said, 'Well, why don't you try to get your paper to finance your — call it a sabbatical or a professional leave of absence type deal.' So that's what I did.

I went to the managing editor and said, 'Jack Anderson has offered me an internship down there to learn how to be an investigative reporter, and learn the tricks of the trade from really the grandfather of investigative journalists.' (The editor) went to the publisher, got a paid leave of absence, which was extremely generous, and I took off. That summer of 1985, I worked for ten weeks for Jack Anderson . . . worked six, seven days a week, I mean ten hours a day, turned out ten columns for them . . . and that's as good as any of the staffers working there did then. I got leaks of incredible material . . . Some stories made quite a splash with the old man, Jack, including one about a congressional junket into the Mediterranean. I got a bunch of cables from a source I developed. And while I was there, it dawned on me that this was an ideal job. These guys had the best job in the world. They covered whatever they liked. They always got stimulating tips. So I started to think about how to parlay the internship into a job.

"I realized they had a lot of interns previously, and they probably had interns banging on their door looking for jobs all the time. I just tried to promote myself by showing my work product, bringing it in, talking to people — not being a pest, but bringing the editors into the story, telling them what devices I used to get particular documents and getting them excited about my work. They knew exactly what I was doing without my having to ask for a lot of guidance. They knew I was interested in moving on. My last week, I did sit down with Jack. I just wanted to thank him, and I told him I realized there weren't any positions open, but I'd be more than willing to scramble for it one day if any positions opened up. That was the only overture I made.

"I continued looking for jobs elsewhere. I just kept in touch with the folks at Jack Anderson, sent them clips. I actually went after stories that had that Jack Anderson imprint — broke a story on how the Board of Selectmen in Framingham and the Board of Public Works violated the (Massachusetts) Open Meeting Law by meeting with a developer over dinner over a development that he had proposed but hadn't yet brought to the Planning Board, all without public notice. I threw into the story things like what they ate, and how much caviar costs on the menu. I interviewed the maitre d' about what kind of restaurant this was.

"And then I found out that Jack was going to be speaking

at Wellesley College. I called up his secretary — whom I liked a great deal; she has red hair and I have red hair, and we got along very well — and asked if Jack could take an early flight and maybe talk to my newspaper. I thought that would benefit my newspaper, and I also thought it would be nice to talk to Jack again, not to pitch a job at him at all.

"I drove him to his hotel room, where he registered. Then I drove him out to the newspaper. He ended up talking to about thirty or forty reporters, gave a rousing speech — you know, his first amendment speech, threats of libel. Then I drove him to his speech that night. All the while, just talking shop and kind of getting to know him.

"He was the one who brought up the job. He said he just didn't have any openings.

"It was in February of '86 that a job did open up there and they asked me . . . if I wanted to write for no byline and no money (laughing). I said, 'Yeah, let me think about it for ten seconds.' "

TIPS FOR WINNING AN INVESTIGATIVE REPORTER'S JOB

"The thing is, I don't really consider myself an investigative reporter. You'll see ads in *E & P* for investigative reporters, and they're looking for somebody aggressive, somebody who won't back down, etc., etc. — all the traits of a good reporter. I think you can be an investigative reporter on the lowest cop beat. You can employ the same tactics . . . that you employ on Capitol Hill or in the White House. Things are what you make of them.

"At *The Middlesex News,* I covered nine different towns. It seemed like at every town I went to something was being covered up. And there was some group in town — whether it was a minority member of the Board of Selectmen, or an environmental group — who was trying to get that out, and didn't know how. You sit down and talk to these people. My first one was in Millis. They had carbon tetrachloride in the water supply. Man, we turned that town on its head, and rightfully so. The Board of Health knew about the problem, had not told the public and was waiting for the state to tell them it was a problem. All I had to do was go to a couple of toxicologists at some universities to find out it could cause stomach cancer.

"I'm a big fan of the internship. There are a lot of internships out there. We have people who come to us who quit paying jobs and come and work for nothing. And then they go out and they've got some national reporting experience. They've got a leg up.

"If they do a good job at an internship, the people who work with them, I think just about anywhere, will help them get placement somewhere. We've placed people in jobs at good newspapers.

"Internships aren't that hard to come by, if you just persevere, and if you're willing to work for nothing."

JOB: Reporter with *The Reston (VA) Times*, a weekly newspaper

NAME: Claudia Gelzer

AGE IN 1988: 22

HOMETOWN: Winston-Salem, NC

EDUCATION: Graduated with degree in journalism from University of Maryland in 1987. Reporter at campus newspaper. Interned at *Greensboro (NC) News and Record*.

HOW DID YOU GET THE JOB?

"I was about a month out of school. I had been sending out resumés and things but I really hadn't had much luck, and really wasn't looking too intensely at that point. I was up in the University of Maryland career center and I saw that there was an opening for a business editor at *The Reston Times* and Times Newspapers.

"I hadn't any business background, but I thought it would be worth a try to . . . do an interview just to get the experience. I called up (the editor) and he said, 'Let's do an interview,' and he set it up for me. I really wasn't qualified for that kind of position, but he was in a situation where he really needed someone fast. He said he'd be willing to teach me. I certainly didn't know how to lay out a page, I wasn't much of a headline writer. I wasn't into any kind of editing — didn't know anything about that kind of thing, but I could have done the reporting end of it.

"I had probably sent stuff out to only about ten or twelve different places, in that range, anything from magazines to dailies to weeklies. I had a couple of interviews, actually, one at a weekly and one at a twice weekly. I got two offers that I declined. One was in southern Maryland. There really wasn't much going on there. I really had hopefully wanted to start on a daily. But if I was going to start on a weekly, I wanted to be near Washington, near some action. So I turned down a position there and one down near Delaware — both in really small, tiny towns.

"I had big conversations with my father about turning these jobs down. He was trying to play devil's advocate, saying, maybe you shouldn't be too hasty in your decisions. But I thought, if I couldn't get a job on a daily, at least I wanted to be in an area where there was a lot going on. In Reston, there's a lot going on there, mostly because it's right near Washington. And so I thought I would take either one or the other — a daily in a small town, or a weekly in a bigger town.

"I had worked at the University of Maryland at the newspaper. I didn't have a whole lot of clips. I probably had about fifty. So I went through and I picked out what I thought were my best five. I listed all my experience in newspapers as internships. I listed the *Diamondback*, and my work at the *News and Record*. I had worked on a community newspaper in Greenbelt, MD. I listed all of that stuff. I (included) a cover letter and five clips. If I was writing to a magazine I would send more feature stuff. If I was writing to a newspaper, the hard news.

"I really came out to this interview just to get the experience. When I saw the newspaper . . . I was pretty impressed. It was a full-color paper and it looked like a real newspaper, and I'd always thought of weeklies as kind of like shoppers.

"I went in for an interview with the business editor, and I told him, you know, I really don't know anything. He said, 'I'm willing to teach you.' It turned out between the time I came for that interview and my second interview, another position came open, and that was a reporter position covering Reston. He said, 'I think this is much more appropriate for you. Are you interested?' And I said yes, and I got the job.

"Maybe another reason (the editor) gave me the job is that I called him every other day and reminded him. Sometimes he'd be on deadline and say, 'I can't talk now. Give me a call back.' And I would. And I just kept calling back, and I kept calling back until I got a second interview. That might have had a lot to do with it. I just think people who are looking for jobs sometimes don't understand why they're not called back right away. And it isn't because, maybe, they're not good. It's just because people are busy, and when they're actually working, they don't always have time. And they don't always remember you. You've got to keep reminding people who you are, and that you really are eager to start.

"I really wanted to start working. I didn't want to waste any time. He told me (the job entailed) long hours because of the small staff and a lot of night work. I told him I was willing to really, really work hard for a year, just put a lot of things aside to get this experience, kind of give up any social life. I was real eager."

(Internships were valuable, she says.) "You know, I had an internship at a supplement of a bigger newspaper and I got to do some writing. But I really wasn't in the news room atmosphere, because it was more a feature supplement. When I got the second internship at the *News and Record*, I was on the copy desk. And that really wasn't what I wanted to do, but it was good to see the environment. It was really fast paced. I was running back and forth, taking copy to the production room, and that kind of thing. I was doing real clerical kind of stuff, but I got to understand deadlines and that kind of thing. I got to meet the type of people that I deal with a lot now. I think news room people are a different breed, and I got to meet a lot of those people."

TIPS FOR LANDING A FIRST REPORTING JOB

"I think you should interview as many places as possible. And just be real persistent. That's what I was with this job."

JOB: Former copy editor with the *Los Angeles Herald Examiner*

NAME: Christopher Nerney

AGE WHEN GOT JOB: 29

HOMETOWN: Franklin, MA

EDUCATION: Graduated from Babson College, 1977, with a B.A., majoring in marketing and communications. Working on master's degree in fiction screen writing at Stanford University.

FIRST JOB: General assignment reporter, *Milford (MA) Daily News*

HOW DID YOU LAND A JOB IN COPY EDITING?

"My first job in journalism was as a general assignment reporter for the *Milford Daily News,* circulation 16,000-something, a small daily in Massachusetts. I was really pushing hard for full-time work, and I had sort of a mentor on the inside — an editor. I went into the office one day, and she sent me up to the editor. I asked him about full-time employment. He put his arm around my shoulder and said he didn't think anything was going to be coming up for at least a year or so. A week later this woman sent me a note that said, don't go get a job as a security guard or anything, because something might be happening here. Two weeks later, I was working full-time.

"A lot of it is timing. You want to be in the right place at the right time. But a function of timing is persistence. You've got to get out there and have contacts. The more contacts you have, the more likely it is that timing will work in your favor."

(Nerney then used his experience at the Milford paper to land a night editor's job at *The Middlesex News,* a larger Massachusetts daily.) "At Milford . . . I was a general assignment reporter, but in the morning I was the wire editor. It was one of those deals, right? You get to throw that on your resumé.

"A copy editing job was attractive. It's seen as a promotion of sorts. You get paid more, you're an editor now, it sort of puts you on the inside. You're there every day around people you're trying to impress. At *The Middlesex News* I was assistant night editor, a job nobody would want, and a job that ruined my social life for one year. You go in at midnight and work till 9:30 — that's going to kill you after awhile. But I thought that might pay off. And it did. I got offered a bureau chief's job, and from there I became assistant metro editor."

(After three years there, he wanted a new challenge. Nerney was accepted to a graduate program at Stanford University in screen writing.) "While I was at Stanford, I realized I had to find some work to stay on the West Coast. I had no contacts on the West Coast, none at all. So my best bet was to mount a very methodical, thorough search of job possibilities on the West Coast. I identified southern California as the best area. There are just tons of really good-sized newspapers in the L.A. area — ten or twelve, anyway, with circulations over 100,000.

"So, I called all these and asked if the editor listed in *E & P* (the *Editor and Publisher Year Book*) was still the editor, and who should I send my resumé to. I did my resumé myself. I mailed them all. I followed up with phone calls. I tried to get interviews. And I ended up having interviews with over half a dozen of the papers.

"It was sort of common knowledge in journalism that copy editors are really in high demand. I thought that would be my best bet, especially since I had copy editing and layout experience.

"During a spring break at Stanford I drove down to Los Angeles and interviewed with as many papers as I could. I had sent resumés maybe six weeks before, followed up with phone calls, told them I'd be down in the area and told them I would call once I got in the area. I did that. I got an interview with the *Herald*, I got an interview with *The Orange County Register*, the (Long Beach) *Press Telegram*.

"It's very important, by the way, to be there. It's hard to get a job on the West Coast when you're over on the East Coast. You have to have a physical presence. They want to be able to meet the person. A lot of these papers want to have tryouts where they see how you're going to do for a week or two.

"I sort of sold myself (with the *Herald Examiner*) with my background. I had at least three years' solid experience on a desk. I had done copy editing and headline writing, all the kind of things that you end up having to do working on a desk at a newspaper.

"In the interview . . . you do all the little things that you take for granted: you dress up, you shave — all those dumb little things that you take for granted, but some people who probably have a problem finding employment don't take for granted. You know, they don't shave. They wear sneakers into the interview."

(Nerney returned in July at the editor's invitation for a full-scale tryout.) "The tryout essentially was you'd go in there and you were a copy editor. They'd spend one night showing you how to work the computer system and the various codes that you have to learn when you're writing headlines, etc. It was sort of humbling, because you'd be sending your headlines and the stories you edited to this common computer file. The guy who was deciding my fate would be looking at them, and if he didn't like it he'd say out loud, 'This headline sucks.' You needed kind of a thick skin.

"You try to put your best foot forward, even though at the time I was living on the beach in California, living out of my tent. I didn't have any money. I left Stanford with $143 and some change, a one-week tryout at the *Herald* and no place to stay down in Los Angeles. I didn't even know anybody in Los Angeles. So I stretched out my money as much as possible, and the best way I was able to do that was to sleep at this tent site on the Pacific Coast Highway in Malibu for $14 a night. You couldn't get a hotel room in Los Angeles for under $30, and the things in the $30 price range were the kind where you sleep with a baseball bat in your bed because the guys that you can hear through the paper-thin wall on the other side are speaking about drugs, and you're worried they're going to bump you off. The camp had the showering facilities. They had picnic tables outside where I ironed my clothes." (Nerney won the job after one week of his tryout, but had to keep living cheaply until he could garner enough money for a down payment on an apartment.) "The fifth week, I couldn't even afford the $14 a night, and what I started to do was sleep in my car. I'd work 5 p.m. to 1 a.m. The last week, I would just park on the side of the road right across the street from where the tent site was. This was one in the morning. At six in the morning, the trucks started rolling by, and they'd shake my car. I always lived in fear that I'd be sleeping, and somebody would go out of control and hit my car on the side of the road, and I'd get killed in my sleep. In the mornings . . . I would sneak up the back way through the scrub brush and the little lizards. I'd take a shower and do everything.

"There was an adventurous aspect to it. You'd get home to the tent at 1:15 in the morning. The moon would be rising over the Pacific. I liked that. I got tired of it by the third week (laughing). You've got to be prepared to suffer some adversity . . . but I tend to think people who want to get into journalism would be that way anyway."

TIPS FOR LANDING A COPY EDITING JOB

"It's probably harder than ever to get a job in journalism; that would be my guess. If you're going for an editing job, get some experience, even if it's at a rinky-dink newspaper. You don't want to manufacture a resumé, but anything you can get on there that's legit, get on there. It looks good in black and white: Wire editor, *Milford Daily News*.

"Another key is to keep calling them. No one's going to call you, unless you're some sort of superstar. And if you're a superstar, you probably didn't have to launch a job hunt, anyway. Try to remember, it's good to ask — especially in the newspaper business — what is a good time to call somebody. A lot of people are on deadline, and they're less receptive to talking to you. It's basically showing a little smarts and some understanding of their job. It's consideration.

"Be there. They're not going to fly you out for a copy editing job. They'll fly you out if you're applying for the managing editor's job. But not for a copy editing job. Be there.

"I encourage any kind of connections. If you have a name to give somebody, it always helps. When I was an editor, I had people calling me up and pitching me stories. If they dropped a name of somebody I know, one of my friends, I'm going to listen to them — more so than if some stranger calls, under deadline. Then I'm going to get rid of them. But if it's somebody who knows somebody I know, even if I'm too busy to talk with them at the time, I'll call them back myself. Because that's the way it is."

JOB: Staff writer, *Time* magazine

NAME: Edward W. Desmond

AGE IN 1988: 30

HOMETOWN: Newton, MA

EDUCATION: Graduated in 1980 from Emerson College, B.A., major in English. Master's degree in law and diplomacy from Fletcher School of Law and Diplomacy at Tufts University, 1982.

FIRST JOB IN JOURNALISM: Full-time stringer, *Cape Cod Times*

HOW DID YOU GET WHERE YOU ARE TODAY?

"The way I got interested (in journalism and foreign affairs) in the first place was traveling in Northern Ireland during the summer of 1979 and living in Belfast for awhile, and doing a lot of photography, which I was interested in at the time, and writing a very extensive article on life in the working-class neighborhoods of Belfast. That was published in *The Boston Globe's* Sunday magazine.

"I knew I really liked writing. I also liked foreign affairs quite a bit.

"This is where the lucky rabbit's foot comes in. When I was at Fletcher, I edited their academic journal in international affairs called the *Fletcher Forum*. One of the people who was helping us was the publisher of *Foreign Affairs*, Doris Forest.

"Not long after school got out — this was in the summer of 1982 — I wrote her a letter thanking her for all her help. Just about the same time she got a call from the office of Henry Grunwald, who was editor-in-chief of *Time*, asking whether she knew of anybody who could come to New York and undertake some research for Grunwald, who was writing a major speech on foreign policy. It turned out that Grunwald's usual researcher, a retired senior editor at *Time*, had an eye problem and couldn't do any reading. Doris Forest had my letter on her desk, and she said, 'I don't know. Maybe this guy would be interested.' And so they gave me a ring.

"I was, in fact, waiting to join the foreign service and not very happy about it. They said, 'Well, you can come to New

York and make a lot of money sitting around doing research for Grunwald,' and I said, 'Sure.'

"I spent seven weeks doing a very extensive research job. He liked it. And I said, 'I want to be a journalist and work at *Time*.' And they said, 'Well, you're not exactly a journalist rich in experience, son. If you're serious, why don't you go out and get a job on a daily, and we'll see what we can do.' But there were no promises at all."

(From 1982 to 1984, Desmond worked as a stringer — getting paid per story — for the *Cape Cod Times*. He also wrote freelance sports feature pieces and other stories for *The Boston Globe*, and returned to New York periodically to do more research projects for Grunwald. He wrote some editorial pieces for the *National Review*. "It didn't go very well. They didn't like my writing . . . It was really quite heartbreaking at the time." Strapped for funds, he lived for a time at his parents' home on Cape Cod.)

"What I learned at Fletcher was really quite invaluable, because I got a basic foundation in the stuff of national and international news reporting: a very good foundation in diplomatic history, international law, economics, the international monetary system, foreign policy generally, security. So I was pretty conversant with all that stuff, which is why I think it went well with Grunwald.

"The difficulty is leapfrogging — sometimes the years involved in getting from a small daily to national and sometimes international coverage. Your education is an enormous benefit, but you have to show you're a reporter.

"(At the *Cape Cod Times*) for awhile I had a beat for the town of Yarmouth, covering school board hearings, writing three stories a day, going in at nine and coming home at midnight. The *Cape Cod Times* is actually a great paper for somebody who is aggressive and wants to be a stringer, because they'll just give out assignments. If you worked for a week on a long feature — fifty bucks — but the incentive was to cover lots of little stories if you needed money. In fact, I kind of changed what I was doing, depending on how I was financially. I could knock off three small news stories in a day sometimes and make seventy-five bucks."

(Eventually, he used his clips to help win a job at *The Middlesex News* in Framingham, MA, a slightly larger circulation daily.) "I had an enormous number of clips by then, covering everything from murders to features. I had won an award for business writing. I had the clips that you need, basically, to prove that you're up to doing daily journalism. I had discovered by then that, even if it's a very small paper, you ask them for a job and they say, 'Well, where's your experience with a daily?' Where am I going to begin if you don't give me a job? That's how I eventually got around that. I guess the central lesson of my experience is that you have to pile up such a lot of clips that they couldn't spring that question on you.

"I was surprised about three and a half months later when *Time* magazine offered me a job as a reporter-researcher. Before I became a staff writer, I had to go through what they call a writer's trial. If you ask for it, and people think you're up to it, they'll give you a writer's trial as a reporter-researcher. That lasts between six and nine months. Mine began, I think, in August of 1985, and I got the go-ahead to be a staff writer in March of 1986. They don't want to commit themselves to hiring you. In fact, it can be somewhat of a nerve-wracking experience. They just put you in a section and you get normal assignments. You get a certain amount of guidance. They have what they call your mentor, and he looks over your work every few weeks. If he sees anything obviously going wrong, he tries to help you out. The people who actually make the decision on whether you pass or fail are the editors for whom you write. They give you a thumbs up or thumbs down."

TIPS FOR JOURNALISTS ASPIRING TO REPORT FOR A TOP NEWS ORGANIZATION

"If you want to stand out a little bit among a large number of very talented people at all levels, whether it's a small weekly or a big daily, the thing to have is some particular specialty, an area in which you're conversant, whether it's economics, or some aspect of politics, or religion, or languages. It gives you a special lock on expertise. Whether you learn it at school, or you develop it just by reading about it, or writing about it, maybe in specialty publications. It gets you a little attention, makes you sound like, or at least pretend, you're an expert.

"I don't think you should specialize right away in the reporting you do. I think the discipline of reporting all of the little stories that are the main staple of a small local paper is extremely good. You know everybody who is young is impatient to cover the big stories. I was very impatient to get on to them. But I don't ever now regret, no matter how mundane it was, the time I spent covering the little stuff.

"It was really kind of fun. You have to learn how to be a writer and a reporter, and that takes time. I liked the *Cape Cod Times* and *The Middlesex News* quite a bit because the desk editors were good, and helped me quite a bit now that I'm at a bigger operation.

"The other thing that I think is really crucial and sets reporters apart is just loving the story. If you see a lot of stories and things, tell people I want to do this story, that story. If you're really enthusiastic about stories, editors like that. That's what it's all about."

JOB: Television producer, CBS-TV's "West 57th St."

NAME: Jane Stone

AGE IN 1988: 29

HOMETOWN: Malone, NY

EDUCATION: Graduated with degree in political science from State University of New York at Binghamton in 1980. Was editor of campus newspaper and worked as a disk jockey at the campus radio station.

FIRST JOB: Editor of *Public Citizen,* a quarterly magazine founded by Ralph Nader

HOW DID YOU GET WHERE YOU ARE TODAY?

"I was editor of the campus newspaper and I met Ralph Nader. Also, the previous editor of the newspaper had just gone to work for him. It was a combination of contacts and good timing (in landing a job as editor of the quarterly magazine, *Public Citizen*).

"I was with the Nader group for about two years, but I did a lot of freelance writing as well. I wrote for *The Nation, The National Law Journal, The Progressive* and the *Washington Journalism Review.* That's how I got my next job, with States News Service (a Washington-based news service). The freelance work caught the (editor's) eye. The freelancing was essential because it expanded on my base with Nader. It gave me some different credentials.

"I worked for States for a little over a year covering Washington issues for Florida papers and then went to work as a Washington correspondent for *The Florida Times-Union.* I had written for Florida papers and knew the Florida contingent in Washington. That's how I got the job. They knew my work. I did that for a year and then I went into television.

"I had been trying to do it for awhile, break into television. It was a very difficult transition. I sent a lot of resumés out. But a person from CBS called me to ask me about a story I had written for the Florida papers. They were doing a similar story. I made a contact, who ultimately went to work for 'Frontline,' (the Public Broadcasting System news program). The contact helped me get a freelance job with 'Frontline.' He remembered me because I had helped him on the story.

"I started out as an associate producer for 'Frontline.' I was able to skip the researcher phase because of my newspaper work. Pretty quickly, I produced some documentaries for PBS. It was all freelance, but I got a lot of exposure jumping from project to project. Ultimately, I got a job on staff (at PBS).

"Then I got a job as a senior producer for WUSA-TV, the CBS affiliate in Washington. I won a few awards there and got some more exposure and attention. Then I got the job as a producer for 'West 57th St.' I did it totally cold. I sent a cover letter and resumé and I got a call shortly thereafter."

TIPS FOR BREAKING INTO TELEVISION

"It's a major transition. Just plug away and make as many contacts as possible. And be persistent. I took a dare because I left my full-time newspaper job for a freelance position. I did it because I really wanted to make it."

JOB: Part-time college journalism instructor; part-time magazine editor

NAME: Brian Kelly

AGE IN 1988: 53

HOMETOWN: Charlottesville, VA

EDUCATION: Graduated from Yale University in 1957. Majored in English.

FIRST JOB: Trainee on copy desk at the *Richmond Times-Dispatch*

HOW DID YOU GET WHERE YOU ARE TODAY?

"I had a B.A. in English and I wanted a job in the writing field so I decided to try journalism. I walked into the *Richmond Times-Dispatch* straight out of college and asked if they had any openings. They gave me three test stories to write and they put me in a training program. I sat on the copy desk for about six months. And I would have stayed there for a year or two but a job opportunity came up in Harrisonburg, VA. The *Times-Dispatch* told me about it because they wanted a stringer up there. So they in effect farmed me out to Harrisonburg, so I got to be a reporter right away. And I was a stringer for the *Times-Dispatch*."

Kelly later took a job with *The Richmond News Leader,* but applied to *The Washington Star* shortly thereafter.

"I sent them my resumé and clips, but I hadn't heard anything back. So I decided to breeze in one day unannounced. I saw the city editor. He took me into his office and said he thought he remembered my name but couldn't remember why. He said, 'Let me look in my drawer.' He had that drawer full of letters. There was one huge stack and one small stack. Looking at the big stack, he said, 'These are the ones I'm sending back. The reason I didn't answer you is because I'm interested in you.'"

Kelly worked for the *Star* for sixteen years and won several local and national journalism awards for his coverage of Virginia politics and events. But in 1978 he decided to try to freelance for a living.

"Things were beginning to circle around and come back again in terms of what I was covering. I felt like I had been there before . . . So I was going to write thriller novels and great things and make a lot of money. But none of that panned out. So after two years of pounding away in the basement on novels and short stories, I decided to try teaching journalism part-time. I had a friend who was teaching journalism (at the University of Virginia) part-time and wanted to take a semester off. So she introduced me to the chairman here and I signed on . . . It's very rewarding. I teach news writing. It keeps my hand in the journalism pot, but it also gives me the freedom to do my own thing. The only drawback is that when a college has a budget crunch, they tend to lop off part-timers. Once when they decided to make some cuts, I applied for a job as an editor with a magazine to make ends meet. That has worked out just fine. I am working thirty hours a week with the magazine and I'm still teaching." (Kelly is a part-time editor with Empire Press, a Virginia company that publishes several history magazines.)

TIPS FOR GETTING INTO TEACHING JOURNALISM

"They should just go to the nearest school and see the appropriate department chairman and talk about it. They have their experience to offer. If they don't have a graduate degree, they do have the experience. Now, some schools require a graduate degree, but some will grant you an exemption . . . Someone should not feel shy about offering his services because he doesn't have to be an educational specialist to teach."

JOB: Press secretary to the governor of Texas

NAME: Jay Rosser

AGE IN 1988: 32

HOMETOWN: Dallas, Texas

EDUCATION: Graduated from Texas Tech University in 1978. Majored in journalism. Minored in political science. Worked on the campus newspaper and had one summer internship at the *Waco Tribune-Herald* in Texas.

FIRST JOB: Reporter for the *Corpus Christi (TX) Caller-Times,* a daily newspaper owned by Harte-Hanks Communications

HOW DID YOU GET WHERE YOU ARE TODAY?

"At one point, Harte-Hanks had a training program. It was designed to be a ten-week course. You spent one week covering county government, one week covering sports, one week in photography. You did a little of everything. If you did real good, you wound up at the flagship paper in Corpus Christi. That was a pretty good deal.

"When I was in my final year in college, I heard about the program through a friend. He invited me out to his home. And he introduced me to a friend of his whose dad was a senior vice president of Harte-Hanks. His dad asked me to send him my resumé. So I sent him my resumé and he called and interviewed me and said I could enter the program . . . The contact paid off."

Rosser was hired by the *Caller-Times* after completing the training program. He worked for the Texas newspaper for about three years when he was promoted to Harte-Hanks' state capital bureau in Austin.

"You have to make a certain commitment to get the attention of others. I was willing to work late. I showed up and offered my assistance when I heard about a major news story — even if I was not scheduled to work. People appreciate that."

Rosser was in the Austin bureau for four years when a Harte-Hanks executive asked him to be editor of a new company-owned Sunday magazine. He worked there until the magazine folded ten months later. He became editor of another Harte-Hanks publication, but soon decided that he wanted a new challenge. Rosser accepted an offer to be deputy press secretary for Governor Bill Clements of Texas.

"I was always fascinated by politics. I sent one resumé to (Clements' office) and fortunately caught somebody's eye. I thought they (Clements' staff) might want to take advantage of my previous experience. As it happens, they were looking for somebody who had contacts with the capital press corps, which I had after four years in Austin. It was a lucky break.

"The thing that fascinated me about journalism was that it was a different story every day. It was never boring. But things had finally reached the point where it was no longer the case. Everything started to look the same. I wanted a new challenge."

TIPS FOR GETTING A MEDIA JOB IN POLITICS

"If you want to do that, you have to decide what avenue you want to take. If you want to go into politics, you have to get that kind of background. See your editor and say you want to cover politics. If you're a sports reporter, it will be hard to go into political work. You don't have the background and qualifications they're looking for."

JOB: Newsletter editor and reporter, Business Publishers, Inc., Silver Spring, MD

NAME: Elizabeth Lohr

AGE IN 1988: 26

HOMETOWN: St. Louis, MO

EDUCATION: Graduated in 1983 from Trinity University (San Antonio, TX), B.A., major in English. Master's degree from University of Missouri, 1985.

FIRST JOB: *The Morning Herald* (Hagerstown, MD)

HOW DID YOU LAND A JOB IN NEWSLETTERS?

"In the (University of Missouri) journalism program, I had been a (Washington) correspondent for a small Missouri paper, the St. Joseph *Gazette*. I just kept track of what was going on on Capitol Hill with the two Missouri senators and the congressman from the district.

"After that, the logical thing to do with a degree in journalism was to try to get on with a daily newspaper. I got on with *The Morning Herald* in Hagerstown.

"I was in Hagerstown for a year, was an education reporter/ features writer. Also, I was a general assignment person. I did fill in on the cops and court beat with whatever needed to be done. After a year I decided that, mainly, I didn't want to live in a small town anymore. I wanted to get back to Washington.

"Actually, I think that was very good experience for what I ended up doing. I ended up going back to being a Washington reporter. I came back from Hagerstown with daily journalism experience and decided to see what I could make happen in newsletters.

"I (landed a temporary job as) a consultant for Thompson Publishing, and I worked on a worker 'right to know' newsletter. Actually, I was only supposed to be there three weeks, but it turned out to be three months. At that point, I was looking around for another job.

"It was obvious there wasn't any permanent position, but the boss that I had there was able to tell me about BPI (Business Publishers, Inc.) and a few other places. He had an inside knowledge about what was going on at BPI — the hiring, firing situation. You need to find people who know what's going on, and it was very difficult to get into that . . . Once you get into the newsletter circuit, it's sort of easy to move around.

"I went up and interviewed at Business Publishers. They saw that I had prior Washington reporting experience. Plus, the daily newspaper stuff really helped. They knew if I could do daily, I could certainly do bimonthly. It was sort of like an automatic in.

"(For clips,) I took what were most likely to be classified as environmental clips from *The Morning Herald.* I had covered a whole series of articles about asbestos in the schools, so I was able to use that to show I wasn't a total stranger to (federal regulatory agencies) and asbestos, and all that. One good thing about being on a daily newspaper is that you can be a generalist — which gives you clips in every area that you can use for any situation you might apply for later. Whereas if you start off in newsletters, say in environment, all you've got is environment clips.

"(The newsletter job) is a very independent situation. I am my own editor and staff. I like that independence. Nobody is really breathing down my neck. On the other hand, I don't get the guidance that I did at a daily newspaper. I don't have an editor saying, 'Hey, this ought to be up higher,' or, 'Think about doing this,' or, 'Did you call so and so?' I pretty much have to be my own boss. Who knows? Maybe it will keep me from getting better.

"But I like the fact that I make a heck of a lot more money than I used to at a small daily newspaper. And it's basically an eight-hour job, which a daily newspaper job was not. And I appreciate that. What I pretty much decided was the kind of writing I like to do best is fiction writing, or freelance, the type of in-depth things with more of a personality angle to them. The job I do is basically for my bread and butter. It's a situation I find likeable, but it's not the be-all and end-all of my writing. It's a good situation for me to be in, because it allows me to look into other things I might want to do, whereas while I was at a daily newspaper that was all I could do, especially in a small town. I spent ten hours a day doing that, and there was no time or energy to do anything else.

"I do know I will be much better off having done this (writing about the environment). Right now, I'm doing a newsletter called 'Sludge,' and another called, 'Solid Waste

Report.' So I guess you could call me a specialist in shit and trash. The trash industry is interesting because . . . you can see it, you can understand what a big problem it is, everybody generates garbage. It's not like toxic waste, something that only big, bad companies produce.

"Any time you work in Washington, anybody else in the rest of the country is going to be impressed, no matter what you did. In a lot of cases, I've found it's really no different than a school board meeting in a small town, but it is Washington, it is senators and congressmen. And that will always be to your advantage."

TIPS FOR LANDING A WASHINGTON NEWSLETTER JOB

"There's just a whole newsletter club here that you can move around in.

"It seems like you can start out in newsletters, but I think you are in really good shape if you do get some daily journalism experience. It's just like the basic training ground. I tore my hair out at certain points, but it's like boot camp. Anybody who really wants to get in this field would be at a disadvantage if they didn't have at least a year's exposure to it.

"People come here because they know there are a lot of publications. I found the competition to be tougher than I would have ever thought. I assumed, oh well, I'm a Missouri graduate, that ought to be an in right there. It might make someone decide to call me in for an interview, but it doesn't really matter that much when there are ten times as many people competing for the same jobs.

"It's really, like they say, who you know. Try to make contacts with people who know people. If you're on an interview and don't get the job, don't be disappointed. There are a million different reasons why somebody else might have gotten that job. The best thing you can do is ask that interviewer (after a rejection) if they know of any jobs or where you might go. Use them."

JOB: Manager of foundation relations for a public interest group

NAME: Kim McGuire

AGE IN 1988: 30

HOMETOWN: Chicago, IL

EDUCATION: Graduated from the University of North Carolina with a degree in journalism in 1979. Worked at the campus radio station and the campus newspaper. Had internships with former U.S. Representative John Buchanan in Washington, the Democratic National Committee, and a political consultant firm.

FIRST JOB: General assignment reporter with *The Star* in Wilmington, NC

HOW DID YOU GET WHERE YOU ARE TODAY?

"Both my parents were journalists. My mother was a newspaper reporter for ten years and my father was in the publishing business. So I think that I knew how competitive the business was, that you needed something to hold when you went into your interviews. I tried to get as much experience in college as possible.

"I picked a number of papers around North Carolina that I was interested in and sent them resumés and clips and offered to come and see them. I went on this circuit of interviews (in her final semester). I met with the editors (of *The Star*) in Wilmington and then bugged them. I decided to focus on that paper because it had a reporting staff of fifteen, they seemed to emphasize good writing and had high standards against just getting it out, which I saw a lot of papers do.

"I think I had the range of writing they were looking for, good work experience, references, and one of my favorite journalism professors had gone to the paper to write editorials. He recommended me. So it would not be wholly truthful to say that I was just this sparkling person who stood out from the pack."

McGuire was hired and eventually worked her way up to the position of political reporter covering the U.S. Senate race between Senator Jesse Helms and Governor Jim Hunt.

"I always thought I wanted to cover politics. That was my goal. When I finally got there, it was in the heat of the political season. It was a huge disappointment for me. Part of it was the realization that I wasn't as good at it as I would like to be. I was very good at the breaking stories, the horse race stuff. But I wasn't satisfied with my own ability to get underneath that, to show what it means.

"I was also disappointed in the political system. I was a little naive. I thought there were some great leaders. But when I got in there and found out how things worked . . . I also was having difficulty staying the cool, neutral observer. I really had opinions on everything. So I made a decision that I wanted to do something different. I was a little burned out and I felt I was missing something. So I went back to school."

McGuire enrolled in a liberal arts master's program at Georgetown University. To pay the bills, she took a job as a part-time reporter with *The Washington Post.*

"I worked out a situation where I could work twenty hours a week and only do stories. I did a lot of news and feature stories. I tried to apply for a couple of full-time reporting jobs, but I didn't get them. That was a bit difficult, but I had to remind myself that my time after Wilmington was a time to think, to see how my skills could be applied to another job.

"I wrote down a list of contacts so I could tell them I was looking for a job and they could tell others. John Buchanan was at the top of the list. (Buchanan, the former congressman for whom McGuire interned in college, was chairman of People For The American Way, a public interest group). I kept in touch with him over the years. So I called him and went to lunch with him. He brought me back here (to People For The American Way). I was hired as manager of foundation relations for the organization. It ended up incorporating a lot of writing about current issues and events."

TIPS FOR GETTING INTO PUBLIC POLICY

"Reporting is a wonderful job. You have a license to learn everything. But one feeling that I had about reporting from the start was that it wasn't an end. It was a way to learn some skills, to be accurate, communicate, write clearly. Those skills can be applied to any job.

"I think that after being in journalism for awhile, you should be aware of what your interests are. Go for informational interviews so you can learn about other fields. That's the best thing you can do."

Index